# 101 Things To Do With Eggs

# 101 Things® To Do With Eggs

BY
TONI PATRICK

GIBBS SMITH
TO ENRICH AND INSPIRE HUMANKIND

First Edition
15 14 13 12 11    10 9 8 7 6 5 4 3 2 1

Text © 2011 Toni Patrick
101 Things is a registered trademark of
Gibbs Smith, Publisher and Stephanie Ashcraft

All rights reserved. No part of this book may be reproduced by
any means whatsoever without written permission from the
publisher, except brief portions quoted for purpose of review.

Published by
Gibbs Smith
P.O. Box 667
Layton, Utah 84041

1.800.835.4993 orders
www.gibbs-smith.com

Contributing editor: Stephanie Ashcraft
Printed and bound in Korea
Gibbs Smith books are printed on either recycled, 100% post-consumer
waste, FSC-certified papers or on paper produced from sustainable PEFC-
certified forest/controlled wood source. Learn more at www.pefc.org.

Library of Congress Cataloging-in-Publication Data

Patrick, Toni.
 101 things to do with eggs / Toni Patrick. — 1st ed.
   p. cm.
 ISBN 978-1-4236-0691-8
 1. Cooking (Eggs) I. Title. II. Title: One hundred one things to do
with eggs. III. Title: One hundred and one things to do with eggs.
 TX745.P38 2011
 641.6'75—dc22

                    2010030687

A special thank you to my friends and
family for their love and support—
as well as their taste buds!

# CONTENTS

Helpful Hints 9

### Fried, Poached, & Scrambled

Fried Eggs, Sausages, and Hash Browns 12 • Fried Eggs and Green Chile Sauce 13 • Butter Poached Eggs in Tomato Sauce 14 • Bleu-Mozzarella Poached Eggs 15 • Poached Eggs with Creamy Spinach Sauce 16 • Southern-Style Eggs Benedict 17 • Vegetarian Eggs Benedict 18 • Poached Eggs Italian 19 • Coffee Cup Scramble 20 • Cheesy Fajita Egg Bites 21 • Herbed Tomato Scrambled Eggs 22 • Indian-Style Scrambled Eggs 23 • Syrupy Scrambled Egg Muffins 24 • Wild Rice Scrambled Eggs 25 • Migas 26 • Toni's Eggcellent Breakfast 27

### Frittatas & Omelets

Frittata 30 • Herbed Frittata 31 • Crab and Asparagus Frittata 32 • Tuscan Frittata 33 • Southwestern Sausage Frittata 34 • Broccoli and Cheddar Frittata 35 • Basic Microwave Omelet 36 • Farmhouse Omelet 37 • Eggcellent Omelet 38 • Cheese-Artichoke Omelet 39 • Omelet Rancheros 40 • Greek Omelet 41

### Appetizers & Sides

Egg Pockets 44 • Hot and Sour Egg Drop Soup 45 • Southern-Style Breakfast Cups 46 • Biscuit Quiches 47 • Egg Puffs 48 • Deviled Eggs 49 • Italian Deviled Eggs 50 • Egg Fried Rice 51 • Winter Squash Custard 52 • Mashed Potato Nests 53

### Burritos, Sandwiches, & Wraps

Breakfast Burritos 56 • Green Chile Burritos 57 • Breakfast Bruschetta 58 • Egg Salad Sandwich 59 • Bagel Sandwich 60 • Monster Sub 61 •

*Eggs in a Nest 62 • Mexi Eggs-In-A-Hole 63 • Stuffed Roll 64 • Ham and Cheese Rolls 65 • Oriental Wraps 66 • Southwestern Egg Wraps 67*

## Quiches & Souffles

*Hash Brown Quiche 70 • Italian Quiche 71 • Spinach and Asiago Quiche 72 • Salmon Quiche 73 • Seafood Souffle 74 • Cheese Souffle 75 • Pumpkin Souffle 76 • Cheesy Layered Souffle 77 • Raspberry Blintz Souffle 78*

## Baked, Strattas, & Casseroles

*Egg Puff Brunch 80 • Mexican-Style Eggs-In-A-Nest 81 • Hawaiian Enchiladas 82 • Artichoke Egg Bake 83 • Broccoli and Egg Bake 84 • Spinach-Hash Brown Pockets 85 • Benedict Strata 86 • Ham and Cheese Strata 87 • Sausage and Pepperoni Strata 88 • Seafood Strata 89 • Strata Milano 90 • Spinach and Cheese Croissant Strata 91 • Chili Egg Puff 92 • Quick Egg Casserole 93 • Egg Lasagna 94 • Mexi-Cali Casserole 95 • Peek-A-Boo Eggs 96 • South-of-the-Border Casserole 97 • Quick and Easy Casserole 98 • Sausage Bake 99*

## Family Favorites

*Muffin Pancakes 102 • Cinnamon Bread Custard 103 • Scotch Eggs 104 • Broccoli-Quiche Stuffed Peppers 105 • Mini Breakfast Pizzas 106 • Egg and Ham Boboli with Cranberry Salsa 107 • Zucchini Fritters 108 • Breakfast Rolls 109 • Tasty Parmesan Tidbits 110 • Egg Loaf 111 • Crab and Asparagus Egg Braid with Curry Sauce 112 • French Bread Custard 113*

## Desserts

*Hot Chocolate Souffle 116 • Classic Flan 117 • Bananas Foster Cheese Pie 118 • Cream Puff Dessert 119 • Baked Custard 120 • Frozen Vanilla Custard Ice Cream 121 • Eggnog Bread Pudding 122 • Raspberry-Dark Chocolate Brulee 123 • Vanilla Cremeux 124 • Custard Cup Sundaes 125*

# HELPFUL HINTS

1. Cold eggs work best for frying.

2. You can poach eggs ahead of time. Keep them in cold water until you are ready to serve. To warm the eggs, simply immerse them in hot water for a few minutes.

3. Milk, broth, or tomato juice can be substituted for poaching water.

4. It's best to separate eggs fresh from the refrigerator, however, for mixing, beating, or whipping, the eggs are easier to work with at room temperature.

5. Cured bacon has twice the fat as Canadian bacon.

6. To reduce fat and calories, substitute reduced-fat foods such as skim milk, light or fat-free sour cream, and light or fat-free cream cheese.

7. It is much more cost effective to use fresh garlic than bottled minced garlic. 1 clove garlic equals 1 teaspoon minced garlic.

8. ¼ cup freshly minced onion equals 2 tablespoons dried minced onion.

9. ¼ cup fresh herbs equal 1 tablespoon dried herbs.

10. Steamed fresh or frozen vegetables may be substituted for canned vegetables.

11. As always, be creative! Most ingredients can be adjusted to your own liking.

# FRIED, POACHED, & SCRAMBLED

# FRIED EGGS, SAUSAGES, AND HASH BROWNS

| | |
|---:|:---|
| ¼ pound | **ground sausage** |
| 1 | **medium onion,** diced |
| 5 tablespoons | **butter or margarine,** divided |
| 1 package (30 ounces) | **shredded hash brown potatoes** |
| | **salt and pepper,** to taste |
| 8 | **eggs** |

Cook sausage and onion in large frying pan until the sausage begins to brown; drain grease and set aside.

Melt 3 tablespoons butter in a separate frying pan over medium heat. Cook hash browns for 10 minutes, or until they begin to brown, and season with salt and pepper. Add to sausage pan and toss to mix. Press mixture together into 4 patties and cook over medium heat until patties have cooked through.

Melt remaining butter in a frying pan. Carefully crack 2 eggs into the pan, taking care not to break the yolks. Season with salt and pepper. Cook slowly until the whites of the eggs are set and the yolks are as desired. Repeat with remaining eggs.

Place 2 eggs over each patty and serve. Makes 4 servings.

# FRIED EGGS AND GREEN CHILE SAUCE

| | |
|---:|:---|
| 2 tablespoons | **butter or margarine** |
| 2 | **eggs** |
| 2 tablespoons | **grated cheddar cheese** |
| 4 tablespoons | **green chile sauce,** warmed |

Melt butter in a frying pan over medium heat. Carefully crack eggs into the pan, taking care not to break the yolks. Once the whites of the eggs begin to set, top each yolk with cheddar cheese. Cover and allow cheese to melt. Serve topped with green chile sauce. Makes 1 serving.

# BUTTER POACHED EGGS IN TOMATO SAUCE

| | |
|---:|:---|
| 4 tablespoons | **butter or margarine,** divided |
| | **salt and pepper,** to taste |
| 1½ cups | **water** |
| 16 | **eggs** |
| 1 cup | **tomato sauce,** warmed |

Place ½ tablespoon of butter and a dash of salt and pepper into 8 ramekins. In a large frying pan over medium heat, bring water to a simmer. Place ramekins in the water and allow the butter to melt. Once the butter has melted, break 2 eggs into each ramekin. Cover and continue simmering until the eggs have set. Remove eggs from ramekins, top with tomato sauce, and serve. Makes 8 servings.

# BLEU-MOZZARELLA POACHED EGGS

| | |
|---:|:---|
| 2 | **English muffins** |
| 4 thick slices | **ham** |
| 2 tablespoons | **butter or margarine** |
| ½ cup | **whipping cream** |
| ½ cup | **chicken broth** |
| 2 tablespoons | **flour** |
| ½ cup | **grated mozzarella cheese** |
| ½ cup | **crumbled bleu cheese** |
| 1 teaspoon | **garlic salt** |
| 1 teaspoon | **salt** |
| 4 | **eggs** |

Toast English muffins and set aside. Fry ham in a medium frying pan over medium-high heat until brown. Set aside.

Melt butter in a saucepan over medium heat. Stir in cream, broth, and flour. Once hot, add cheeses and garlic salt. Stir until cheeses are completely melted.

Add enough water to a medium frying pan to measure 1¼ inches. Add salt. Bring water to a simmer over medium heat. Crack eggs 1 at a time and gently slip into water. Cook until egg whites are just set and egg yolks are still runny, about 3 minutes. With slotted spoon, lift out eggs and place on paper towels.

Place 1 slice of ham and 1 poached egg on each half of the English muffins. Top with sauce and serve. Makes 2–4 servings.

# POACHED EGGS WITH CREAMY SPINACH SAUCE

| | |
|---:|:---|
| 2 | **English muffins** |
| 1 cup | **milk** |
| 2 tablespoons | **cream of spinach soup mix** |
| 1 teaspoon | **salt** |
| 4 | **eggs** |
| 4 thick slices | **large tomato** |

Toast English muffins and set aside.

In a small saucepan, bring milk to a simmer. Add the soup mix and simmer another 2 minutes or until sauce thickens.

Add enough water to a medium frying pan to measure 1¼ inches. Add salt. Bring water to a simmer over medium heat. Crack eggs 1 at a time and gently slip into water. Cook until egg whites are just set and egg yolks are still runny, about 3 minutes. With slotted spoon, lift out eggs and place on paper towels.

Place 1 slice of tomato and 1 poached egg on each half of the English muffins. Top with sauce and serve. Makes 2–4 servings.

# SOUTHERN-STYLE EGGS BENEDICT

|   |   |
|---:|:---|
| 4 | **English muffins** |
| 4 | **green chiles,** halved and seeded |
| 1 tablespoon | **olive oil** |
| 8 | **breakfast sausage patties** |
| 4 | **egg yolks** |
| 1 1/2 teaspoons | **salt,** divided |
| 1 tablespoon | **lemon juice** |
| 1/2 cup | **butter or margarine,** melted |
| 1/2 cup | **grated pepper jack cheese** |
| 8 | **eggs** |
| 8 slices | **tomato** |

Toast English muffins and set aside.

In a large frying pan, saute the green chiles in oil over medium heat until softened, about 5 minutes. Set aside. In the same frying pan, brown sausage patties until cooked through.

In a blender, combine the egg yolks, 1/2 teaspoon salt, and lemon juice. With blender running, gradually add hot butter until well mixed. Transfer to a small saucepan and stir in the cheese until melted.

Add enough water to a medium frying pan to measure 1 1/4 inches. Add remaining salt. Bring water to a simmer over medium heat. Crack eggs 1 at a time and gently slip into water. Cook until egg whites are just set and egg yolks are still runny, about 3 minutes. With slotted spoon, lift out eggs and place on paper towels.

Place 1 sausage patty, 1 green chili, 1 slice of tomato, and 1 poached egg on each half of the English muffins. Top with sauce and serve. Makes 4–6 servings.

# VEGETARIAN EGGS BENEDICT

| | |
|--:|:--|
| 4 thick slices | **tomato** |
| 4 thick slices | **eggplant** |
| 1 tablespoon | **olive oil** |
| 2 | **English muffins** |
| 1 teaspoon | **salt** |
| 4 | **eggs** |
| ¼ cup | **pesto,** divided |

Preheat oven to 400 degrees.

Brush tomato and eggplant slices with oil and roast in a preheated oven for 5 minutes, turning once. Toast English muffins and set aside.

Add enough water to a medium frying pan to measure 1¼ inches. Add salt. Bring water to a simmer over medium heat. Crack eggs 1 at a time and gently slip into water. Cook until egg whites are just set and egg yolks are still runny, about 3 minutes. With slotted spoon, lift out eggs and place on paper towels.

Spread 1 tablespoon pesto on each English muffin half. Place 1 slice of tomato, 1 slice of eggplant, and 1 poached egg on each half of the English muffins. Top with pesto and serve. Makes 2–4 servings.

# POACHED EGGS ITALIAN

| | |
|---:|:---|
| 2 slices | **fresh Italian bread** |
| 1/2 cup | **grated mozzarella cheese** |
| 2 | **Roma tomatoes,** diced |
| 1/2 tablespoon | **finely chopped fresh basil leaves** |
| 2 tablespoons | **olive oil** |
| 1 tablespoon | **balsamic vinegar** |
| 1 teaspoon | **salt** |
| 4 | **eggs** |

Preheat oven for broiler.

Place bread on a baking sheet. Divide cheese between slices and spread evenly. Toast under broiler until cheese has melted and begins to brown.

In a small bowl, toss tomatoes with basil, oil, and vinegar.

Add enough water to a medium frying pan to measure 1 1/4 inches. Add salt. Bring water to a simmer over medium heat. Crack eggs 1 at a time and gently slip into water. Cook until egg whites are just set and egg yolks are still runny, about 3 minutes. With slotted spoon, lift out eggs and place on paper towels.

Place 2 poached eggs on each slice of bread. Top with tomato mixture and serve. Makes 2 servings.

# COFFEE CUP SCRAMBLE

| | |
|---:|:---|
| 2 | **eggs** |
| 2 tablespoons | **milk** |
| 2 tablespoons | **grated sharp cheddar cheese** |
| | **salt and pepper,** to taste |

Prepare a 12-ounce microwave-safe coffee mug with nonstick cooking spray. Add eggs and milk; beat until blended. Microwave on high 45 seconds; stir. Return to microwave for another 30–45 seconds, or until eggs have set. Top with cheese; season with salt and pepper. Makes 1 serving.

# CHEESY FAJITA EGG BITES

| | |
|---:|:---|
| 6 | **eggs** |
| ¼ cup | **water** |
| | **salt and pepper,** to taste |
| ½ package (1.25 ounces) | **fajita mix** or to taste |
| 1 tablespoon | **butter or margarine** |
| ½ cup | **diced green bell pepper** |
| ½ cup | **diced red bell pepper** |
| ½ cup | **diced cooked chicken** |
| 1 cup | **grated cheddar cheese** |
| ½ cup | **lightly crushed tortilla chips** |

Beat eggs, water, salt, and pepper in medium bowl until frothy. Stir in fajita mix.

Heat butter in a 10-inch frying pan over medium heat. Add bell peppers to pan and saute until tender. Stir in chicken and mix. Add to egg mixture with cheese and chips. Mix and return to pan. As eggs begin to set, gently pull the eggs across the pan with an inverted turner, forming large soft curds. Continue cooking—pulling, lifting, and folding eggs—until thickened and no visible liquid egg remains. Do not stir constantly. Serve once eggs have completely set. Makes 3–6 servings.

# HERBED TOMATO SCRAMBLED EGGS

| | |
|---:|:---|
| 1 can (14.5 ounces) | **diced tomatoes** |
| 12 | **eggs** |
| 8 ounces | **garlic and herb flavored cream cheese,** softened |
| 2 tablespoons | **butter or margarine** |

Drain tomatoes. Combine eggs and cream cheese and beat until blended.

Melt butter in a large frying pan over medium heat. Add tomatoes to butter and saute until soft. Add egg mixture to tomatoes and mix. As eggs begin to set, gently pull the eggs across the pan with an inverted turner, forming large soft curds. Continue cooking—pulling, lifting, and folding eggs—until thickened and no visible liquid egg remains. Do not stir constantly. Serve once eggs have completely set. Makes 6–8 servings.

# INDIAN-STYLE SCRAMBLED EGGS

| | |
|---:|:---|
| 1/2 cup | **finely chopped onion** |
| 1/2 teaspoon | **minced fresh ginger** |
| 1/4 teaspoon | **ground cumin** |
| 1 | **small tomato,** chopped |
| 1 teaspoon | **minced jalapeno** |
| 4 | **eggs** |
| 1 tablespoon | **chopped fresh cilantro** |
| | **salt,** to taste |

Prepare a large frying pan with nonstick cooking spray and heat over medium heat until hot. Add onion, ginger, and cumin; cook until onion is soft. Add tomato and jalapeno; cook 2 minutes longer.

Beat eggs, cilantro, and salt in medium bowl until blended. Pour over mixture in pan. As eggs begin to set, gently pull the eggs across the pan with an inverted turner, forming large soft curds. Continue cooking—pulling, lifting, and folding eggs—until thickened and no visible liquid egg remains. Do not stir constantly. Serve once eggs have completely set. Makes 2 servings.

# SYRUPY SCRAMBLED EGG MUFFINS

| | |
|---:|:---|
| ½ pound | **pork sausage** |
| 12 | **eggs** |
| ½ cup | **chopped onion** |
| ¼ cup | **chopped green bell pepper** |
| ½ teaspoon | **salt** |
| ¼ teaspoon | **garlic powder** |
| ½ cup | **grated cheddar cheese** |
| ½ cup | **maple syrup** |

Preheat oven to 350 degrees and prepare a 12-cup muffin pan with nonstick cooking spray.

In a frying pan, brown the sausage and then drain. In a large bowl, beat eggs; add onion, bell pepper, salt, and garlic powder. Stir in sausage and cheese. Using a ⅓ cup measure, pour mixture into muffin cups. Drizzle syrup on top of egg mixture. Bake for 20–25 minutes or until a knife inserted into the center comes out clean. Makes 12 servings.

# WILD RICE SCRAMBLED EGGS

| | |
|---:|:---|
| 12 | **eggs** |
| 1/3 cup | **milk** |
| 1 cup | **pre-cooked long-grain wild rice** |
| 6 | **large fresh mushrooms,** sliced |
| 1 | **small green bell pepper,** diced |
| 1/2 cup | **minced white onion** |
| 6 slices | **ham, diced, or two chicken breasts,** cooked and diced |
| | **salt and pepper,** to taste |
| 1 cup | **grated Colby Jack cheese** |
| 1 | **large fresh tomato,** diced |
| | **parsley** |

Preheat oven to 300 degrees and prepare a large and deep ovenproof frying pan with nonstick cooking spray. Heat pan over medium heat until hot.

Beat eggs and combine with milk. Pour into pan, and as eggs begin to set, gently pull the eggs across the pan with an inverted turner, forming large soft curds. Continue cooking—pulling, lifting, and folding eggs—until thickened but not completely done. Do not stir constantly.

Take off burner and stir in rice, mushrooms, bell pepper, onion, ham, salt, and pepper. Mix well. Sprinkle with cheese and top with diced tomatoes and parsley.

Place uncovered pan in oven and bake for 15 minutes. Eggs will finish cooking. Let sit for 5 minutes to set, then cut into 6 pie-shaped portions and serve hot. Makes 6 servings.

# MIGAS

| | |
|---:|:---|
| 2 bunches | **green onions,** chopped |
| 3 tablespoons | **butter or margarine** |
| 12 | **eggs** |
| 1 tablespoon | **cumin** |
| 1 tablespoon | **garlic powder or granulated garlic** |
| 1 tablespoon | **basil** |
| 2 cups | **grated Monterey Jack or cheddar cheese** |
| 2½ cups | **salted tortilla chips,** slightly crumbled |
| 1½ cups | **picante sauce** |

In a frying pan, saute onions in butter. In a large bowl, beat eggs, cumin, garlic, and basil together. Add onions, cheese, tortilla chips, and picante sauce and toss to mix.

Pour into frying pan and cook over medium heat. As eggs begin to set, gently pull the eggs across the pan with an inverted turner, forming large soft curds. Continue cooking—pulling, lifting, and folding eggs—until thickened and no visible liquid egg remains. Do not stir constantly. Makes 6 servings.

# TONI'S EGGCELLENT BREAKFAST

| | |
|---:|:---|
| ½ bag (of 30 ounce package) | **shredded hash brown potatoes** |
| ½ cup | **green bell pepper,** diced |
| ½ cup | **onion,** diced |
| 3 tablespoons | **butter or margarine** |
| 4 | **eggs** |
| | **Mrs. Dash,** to taste |
| | **salt and pepper,** to taste |
| 4 strips | **bacon,** cooked and crumbled |
| ¼ cup | **grated cheddar cheese** |
| ½ cup | **diced tomato** |

In a large frying pan, cook hash browns, bell pepper, and onion in butter.

While hash browns are cooking, beat eggs in a bowl with Mrs. Dash, salt, and pepper. When hash browns are slightly brown, pour the eggs into the pan with the vegetables and add bacon. As eggs begin to set, gently pull the eggs across the pan with an inverted turner, forming large soft curds. Continue cooking—pulling, lifting, and folding eggs—until thickened and no visible liquid egg remains. Do not stir constantly. Once eggs have completely set, add cheese and tomato and lightly toss. Makes 4 servings.

# FRITTATAS & OMELETS

# FRITTATA

| | |
|---:|:---|
| 2½ cups | **shredded hash brown potatoes** |
| | **salt and pepper,** to taste |
| 2 | **eggs** |
| 6 | **egg whites** |
| ½ cup | **crumbled goat cheese** |
| ½ cup | **diced ham** |
| 1 tablespoon | **fresh dill** |
| ¼ cup | **diced roasted red bell peppers** |

Place oven rack on top shelf and preheat oven to 350 degrees.

Over medium heat in a 12-inch ovenproof frying pan prepared with nonstick cooking spray, cook hash browns 5 minutes or until golden brown; season with salt and pepper.

Combine remaining ingredients with a whisk. Pour evenly over potatoes and cook 2 minutes or until edges are set. Place in oven and bake for 8–10 minutes or until the center is set. Makes 6–8 servings.

# HERBED FRITTATA

| | |
|---:|:---|
| 3 | **medium potatoes** |
| 1 tablespoon | **olive oil** |
| 6 | **eggs** |
| 1 teaspoon | **parsley** |
| 1/2 teaspoon | **basil** |
| 1/2 teaspoon | **oregano** |
| | **salt and pepper,** to taste |
| 1 cup | **grated cheddar cheese** |
| 1/2 cup | **diced ham** |
| 1 | **small tomato,** diced |

Place oven rack on top shelf and preheat oven to 375 degrees.

Wash and prick potatoes with a fork. Microwave for 3–4 minutes or until soft. Brush sides and bottom of a large frying pan that has an ovenproof handle with oil. Thinly slice potatoes and use them to cover the bottom of the pan. Cook over medium heat until golden, turning to cook both sides.

Beat eggs in a large bowl. Add spices, salt, and pepper and mix well. Add cheese and ham; mix well and then pour over potatoes.

Cook over medium heat until sides have set, about 5–8 minutes. Place pan in oven and cook until egg mixture is done, about 8 minutes. Top with diced tomatoes and serve immediately. Makes 6–8 servings.

# CRAB AND ASPARAGUS FRITTATA

| | |
|---:|:---|
| 1 cup | **small pieces fresh asparagus** |
| 1 cup | **sliced mushrooms** |
| ½ cup | **sliced green onions** |
| ½ | **red bell pepper,** cut into strips |
| ½ cup | **flaked crab meat** |
| 8 | **eggs** |
| ¼ cup | **water** |
| 1 teaspoon | **dried Italian seasoning** |
| ½ cup | **grated mozzarella cheese** |
| 1 tablespoon | **grated Parmesan cheese** |

Preheat oven to 375 degrees.

Prepare a 10-inch nonstick frying pan with an ovenproof handle with nonstick cooking spray. Over medium heat, saute asparagus, mushrooms, onions, and bell pepper until crisp-tender, about 5 minutes. Remove from heat, add crab, and mix well.

Beat eggs, water, and seasoning in medium bowl until blended. Stir in mozzarella cheese and pour over crab mixture in pan. Cook over medium heat until eggs are set at edges, 5–8 minutes. Sprinkle with Parmesan cheese.

Place in oven and bake until top is lightly browned, eggs are completely set, and no visible liquid egg remains; 8–10 minutes. Cut into wedges. Makes 6–8 servings.

# TUSCAN FRITTATA

| | |
|---:|:---|
| 1 | **small white onion,** diced |
| 2 tablespoons | **extra virgin olive oil** |
| ¾ cup | **chopped fresh baby spinach leaves** |
| ¼ cup | **chopped fresh basil leaves** |
| 9 | **eggs** |
| ¾ cup | **milk** |
| ½ teaspoon | **pepper** |
| ¼ cup | **chopped sun-dried tomato strips** |
| ¼ cup | **chopped roasted red bell pepper strips** |
| 1 cup | **grated mozzarella cheese** |

Preheat oven to 400 degrees.

In a 12-inch ovenproof frying pan over medium heat, saute onions in olive oil. Once they begin to look clear, lower heat slightly to medium-low and add spinach and basil to pan to wilt.

In a bowl whisk together eggs, milk, and pepper. Add this mixture to the pan once the spinach and basil have wilted slightly. Without scraping the bottom of the pan, evenly distribute the egg mixture. Sprinkle tomatoes and bell pepper over the top of the mixture. Continue cooking for about 10 minutes or until the sides of the frittata have set. Sprinkle with mozzarella.

Place in oven and bake for about 15 minutes or until the eggs have puffed up and are cooked through. Makes 8 servings.

# SOUTHWESTERN SAUSAGE FRITTATA

| | |
|---:|:---|
| 1 | **small red bell pepper,** finely chopped |
| 3 | **green onions,** finely chopped |
| 1 tablespoon | **unsalted butter or margarine** |
| 1/2 pound | **sausage** |
| 10 | **eggs** |
| 1/2 cup | **whipping cream** |
| 3 tablespoons | **finely chopped fresh parsley** |
| 3 tablespoons | **coarsely chopped fresh cilantro leaves** |
| 1 teaspoon | **salt** |
| 1/4 teaspoon | **cayenne pepper** |
| | **salsa** |

Preheat oven to 350 degrees.

In a large frying pan over medium heat, saute bell pepper and onions in butter until peppers are limp. Set aside in a small bowl. Add sausage to the pan and cook until sausage is no longer pink. Remove from heat and drain fat.

In a large bowl whisk together eggs, cream, parsley, cilantro, salt, and cayenne pepper. Stir in the sausage mixture.

Prepare a 9 x 13-inch baking dish with nonstick cooking spray. Pour in mixture and bake until the top is golden and the eggs have set, about 30–40 minutes. Allow to cool before serving. Slice frittata into squares and top with salsa. Makes 10–12 servings.

# BROCCOLI AND CHEDDAR FRITTATA

| | |
|---:|:---|
| 1 package (10 ounces) | **frozen chopped broccoli** |
| ¼ cup | **water** |
| 8 | **eggs** |
| ¼ cup | **milk** |
| 2 teaspoons | **mustard** |
| 1 teaspoon | **seasoned salt** |
| ⅛ teaspoon | **pepper** |
| ¾ cup | **grated cheddar cheese** |
| 3 | **green onions,** chopped |

In a large microwave-safe bowl, steam broccoli in water until tender. Drain well and set aside.

Beat eggs, milk, mustard, salt, and pepper in large bowl until blended. Add broccoli, cheese, and onions and mix well.

Prepare a large frying pan with nonstick cooking spray; heat over medium heat until hot. Pour in egg mixture; cook over low to medium heat until eggs are almost set; 8–10 minutes. Remove from heat. Cover and let stand until eggs are completely set, 8–10 minutes. Cut into wedges and serve. Makes 4–6 servings.

# BASIC MICROWAVE OMELET

| | |
|---:|:---|
| 2 | **eggs** |
| 2 tablespoons | **water** |
| 1/8 teaspoon | **salt** |
| | **dash pepper** |
| 1 teaspoon | **butter or margarine** |
| 1/4 cup | **grated cheddar cheese** |
| 3 strips | **bacon,** cooked and crumbled |

Beat eggs, water, salt, and pepper in small bowl until blended.

Microwave butter in 9-inch glass pie plate on high for 30 seconds. Tilt plate to coat bottom evenly. Pour egg mixture into hot pie plate. Cover tightly with plastic wrap, leaving a small vent. Microwave on high 1½–2 minutes or until eggs have completely set, do not stir.

Place cheese and bacon on one half of the omelet. Fold omelet in half and serve immediately. Makes 1–2 servings.

# FARMHOUSE OMELET

| | |
|---:|:---|
| 1½ cups | **chopped onion** |
| 3 tablespoons | **vegetable oil** |
| 4 cups | **cooked and diced potatoes** |
| ¾ cup | **diced fully cooked ham** |
| 12 | **eggs** |
| 3 tablespoons | **minced fresh parsley** |
| 2 teaspoons | **paprika** |
| 1 teaspoon | **salt** |
| ½ teaspoon | **pepper** |
| ½ teaspoon | **garlic salt** |
| ½ teaspoon | **celery salt** |
| 12 | **bacon strips,** cooked and crumbled |

Preheat oven to 400 degrees.

Over medium-high heat in a 12-inch ovenproof frying pan prepared with nonstick cooking spray, cook onion in oil until tender. Add potatoes and ham and cook until hot. Remove from the heat.

In a bowl, beat eggs, parsley, and seasonings. Add to potato mixture and stir gently to mix; fold in bacon. Bake, uncovered, for 20–30 minutes or until a knife inserted near the center comes out clean. Makes 8–10 servings.

# EGGCELLENT OMELET

| | |
|---:|:---|
| 3 | **medium potatoes,** peeled and diced |
| 3 tablespoons | **olive oil** |
| 1 | **medium onion,** diced |
| 1 | **green bell pepper,** diced |
| 1 teaspoon | **minced garlic** |
| | **salt and pepper,** to taste |
| 6 | **eggs** |
| ¼ cup | **milk** |
| ⅓ cup | **freshly grated Pecorino Romano cheese** |

In a large frying pan, saute potatoes in oil. Add onion, bell pepper, and garlic. Continue cooking until all are tender. Season with salt and pepper. Evenly distribute vegetables in pan.

Beat eggs with milk and pour over vegetables. Sprinkle with cheese, cover, and cook over low heat until eggs are set. Flip and cook the other side until golden brown. Fold and serve. Makes 4 servings.

# CHEESE-ARTICHOKE OMELET

| | |
|--:|:--|
| ¾ cup | **salsa** |
| 1 cup | **chopped artichoke hearts** |
| ¼ cup | **grated Parmesan cheese** |
| 1 cup | **grated Monterey Jack cheese** |
| 1 cup | **grated cheddar cheese** |
| 6 | **eggs** |
| 1 cup | **nonfat plain yogurt** |

Preheat oven to 350 degrees.

Prepare a 10-inch quiche dish or pie pan with nonstick cooking spray. Spread salsa over bottom. Distribute artichokes over the salsa. Sprinkle cheeses in layers.

In a medium bowl, beat eggs and yogurt, blending until smooth. Pour egg mixture over cheeses. Bake, uncovered, for 30–40 minutes or until set. Cut into wedges and serve. Makes 6 servings.

# OMELET RANCHEROS

| | |
|---:|:---|
| 1 cup | **refried beans** |
| 1/4 cup | **salsa,** divided |
| 2 | **eggs** |
| 2 tablespoons | **milk** |
| 2 tablespoons | **grated cheddar cheese** |

Mix beans and 2 tablespoons salsa in small saucepan. Cook and stir over medium heat until heated through; keep warm.

Beat eggs and milk in small bowl until blended. Prepare a 7-inch omelet pan or frying pan with nonstick cooking spray; heat over medium-high heat until hot. Pour in egg mixture. Mixture should set immediately at edges.

Gently push cooked portions from edges toward the center with inverted turner so that uncooked eggs can reach the hot pan surface. Continue cooking, tilting pan, and gently moving cooked portions as needed.

When top surface of eggs is thickened and no visible liquid egg remains, spread bean filling down center of omelet; sprinkle with cheese. Fold sides over filling with turner; slide onto plate. Top with remaining salsa. Serve immediately. Makes 1 serving.

# GREEK OMELET

| | |
|---:|:---|
| 1 tablespoon | **chopped red bell pepper** |
| 1 teaspoon | **olive oil** |
| 2 handfuls | **baby spinach** |
| 3 | **eggs** |
| 1 tablespoon | **milk** |
| | **salt and pepper,** to taste |
| 1 teaspoon | **butter or margarine** |
| 1 tablespoon | **chopped black olives** |
| 2 tablespoons | **crumbled feta cheese** |

Using a large frying pan, saute bell pepper in oil until soft. Add the spinach and slightly saute, just until it starts to wilt, and set aside.

In a medium bowl, whisk together eggs, milk, salt, and pepper. Heat an 8-inch frying pan over medium heat. Add butter to coat the pan. Pour in the egg mixture and let stand just until edges begin to cook. Gently lift the omelet with a turner to ensure that the uncooked egg flows underneath.

Place the spinach and bell pepper filling onto one side of the omelet. Then sprinkle the olives and feta on top. Using a turner, very gently lift and fold the omelet in half, making sure to enclose all of the filling inside. Let stand for a few seconds and serve. Makes 1–2 servings.

# APPETIZERS & SIDES

# EGG POCKETS

| | |
|---:|:---|
| 1 can (12 ounces, 10 count) | **refrigerated flaky biscuits** |
| 4 ounces | **cream cheese,** cut into 10 cubes |
| 10 | **eggs** |
| 1 cup | **grated provolone cheese,** divided |
| 1 | **green onion,** sliced |
| ¼ cup | **diced red bell pepper** |
| ¼ cup | **diced yellow bell pepper** |

Preheat oven to 350 degrees and prepare a 12-cup muffin pan generously with nonstick cooking spray.*

Separate biscuits and form each into 6-inch rounds. Place 1 round in each of 10 muffin cups, pressing up and beyond sides. Place a cube of cream cheese in each cup. Gently break an egg into each cup and sprinkle with cheese, onion, and bell peppers. Pinch together biscuit edges tightly to seal.

Bake 20–25 minutes or until biscuits are golden brown. Gently remove from cups and place on serving plates. Makes 10 servings.

*Tip: Fill the empty cups half full with water before baking. This will prevent damage to your pans.

# HOT AND SOUR EGG DROP SOUP

| | |
|---:|:---|
| 2 cans (14 ounces each) | **chicken broth** |
| 1 cup | **frozen peas** |
| 1 can (4 ounces) | **sliced mushrooms,** drained |
| $1/3$ cup | **rice wine vinegar** |
| 1 tablespoon | **soy sauce** |
| $1/2$ teaspoon | **pepper** |
| $1/4$ cup | **cold water** |
| 2 tablespoons | **cornstarch** |
| 4 | **eggs,** beaten |

In a large saucepan, combine broth, peas, mushrooms, vinegar, soy sauce, and pepper. Cook on high heat until mixture comes to a boil. Reduce to medium heat and allow it to simmer for 5 minutes.

Mix water and cornstarch in small bowl until dissolved. Slowly stir into hot soup. While gently stirring soup, slowly stir in eggs. Portion into 4 bowls and serve immediately. Makes 4 servings.

# SOUTHERN-STYLE BREAKFAST CUPS

| | |
|---:|:---|
| 3 | **small flour tortillas,** cut in half |
| 12 | **eggs** |
| 1½ cups | **grated cheddar cheese** |
| 6 strips | **bacon,** cooked and crumbled |
| | **cilantro,** to taste |
| 6 tablespoons | **sour cream** |
| 6 tablespoons | **salsa** |

Preheat oven to 375 degrees. Prepare 6 small souffle dishes generously with nonstick cooking spray.

Place half a tortilla in each dish with flat edge down and wrapped around inside edge of dish to make a bottomless crust. Break 2 eggs in each cup. Evenly distribute cheese between each cup and top with bacon and sprinkle with cilantro.

Bake for 30 minutes or until eggs are done, cheese is melted, and tortilla is slightly brown. Gently remove from dishes and place on serving plates. Top with 1 tablespoon each of sour cream and salsa. Makes 6 servings.

# BISCUIT QUICHES

| | |
|---:|:---|
| ²/₃ cup | **grated Swiss cheese** |
| ¹/₃ cup | **finely chopped thin lunchmeat ham** |
| ¹/₄ cup | **finely chopped green onions** |
| 3 | **eggs** |
| 2 tablespoons | **milk** |
| ¹/₄ teaspoon | **salt** |
| ¹/₈ teaspoon | **pepper** |
| 1 can (12 ounces, 10 count) | **refrigerated flaky biscuits** |

Preheat oven to 350 degrees and prepare a 12-cup muffin pan generously with nonstick cooking spray*.

Combine cheese, ham, and onions in small bowl. In a separate bowl, beat eggs, milk, salt, and pepper until well mixed.

Separate biscuits and form each into 5-inch rounds. Place 1 in each of 10 muffin cups, pressing up and over sides to form the crust. Evenly distribute cheese mixture between the cups and top each with egg mixture, distributed evenly. Bake 20–25 minutes or until eggs have set and biscuits are golden brown. Gently remove from pan and place on serving plates. Makes 10 servings.

*Tip: Fill the empty cups half full with water before baking. This will prevent damage to your pans.

# EGG PUFFS

| | |
|---:|:---|
| 1 package (10 ounces, 6 count) | **frozen puff-pastry shells** |
| 6 | **eggs** |
| ¼ cup | **cream cheese,** softened |
| ¼ cup | **half-and-half** |
| ½ teaspoon | **dried dill weed** |
| | **dash salt** |

Preheat oven to 400 degrees.

Bake pastry shells on baking sheet for 20 minutes. Cut off the tops and set aside. Carefully remove soft dough from centers and discard.

Reduce oven setting to 375 degrees. Break 1 egg into each shell. Bake until whites are almost set, 14–15 minutes.

Mix cream cheese, half-and-half, dill weed, and salt in a small bowl. Evenly distribute cheese mixture between the shells and bake for 3 minutes or until hot. Replace the top from the shell and place on serving dishes. Makes 6 servings.

# DEVILED EGGS

| | |
|---:|:---|
| 6 | **hard-boiled eggs** |
| 4 tablespoons | **ranch dressing** |
| 2 teaspoons | **mayonnaise** |
| ½ teaspoon | **mustard** |
| 1 tablespoon | **minced onion** |
| 2 teaspoons | **minced green bell pepper** |
| | **paprika** |

Shell eggs and cut in half lengthwise. Remove yolks to a small bowl and mash with a fork. Add ranch, mayonnaise, mustard, onion, and bell pepper and stir to combine. Spoon mixture into egg whites. Sprinkle with paprika and serve. Makes 12 servings.

# ITALIAN DEVILED EGGS

|  |  |
|---:|:---|
| 12 | **hard-boiled eggs** |
| 6 | **artichoke hearts** |
| ½ tablespoon | **basil** |
| 1 tablespoon | **grated Asiago cheese** |
| 1 tablespoon | **grated mozzarella cheese** |
| ¼ cup | **finely chopped roasted red bell pepper** |
| 3 tablespoons | **mayonnaise** |
| | **salt and pepper,** to taste |
| | **parsley** |

Shell eggs and cut in half lengthwise. Remove yolks to a food processor and add artichokes, basil, cheeses, bell pepper, mayonnaise, salt, and pepper. Process until smooth and creamy. Spoon mixture into egg whites. Sprinkle with parsley and serve. Makes 24 servings.

# EGG FRIED RICE

| | |
|--:|:--|
| 1 tablespoon | **vegetable oil** |
| 2 teaspoons | **sesame oil** |
| 3 | **eggs** |
| 4 cups | **cooked instant rice** |
| 1 cup | **peas** |
| 1/3 cup | **chopped green onions** |
| 1/4 teaspoon | **salt** |
| 1/4 teaspoon | **pepper** |

Heat vegetable oil in a large nonstick frying pan or wok over medium-high heat.

In a small bowl, beat together sesame oil and eggs. Pour mixture into pan and allow it to cook for 2 minutes, stirring regularly. Mix in rice and cook for another 3 minutes, stirring occasionally. Add peas, onion, salt, and pepper and cook 5 more minutes, stirring occasionally. Serve immediately. Makes 5 servings.

# WINTER SQUASH CUSTARD

| | |
|---:|:---|
| 3 | **eggs** |
| ⅓ cup | **packed brown sugar** |
| ½ teaspoon | **salt** |
| ½ teaspoon | **pumpkin pie spice** |
| 1 can (16 ounces) | **pumpkin** |
| 1 package (12 ounces) | **frozen winter squash,** thawed |
| ¼ cup | **chopped toasted pecans** |

Preheat oven to 350 degrees.

In a large bowl, beat eggs, brown sugar, salt, and spice. Add pumpkin, squash, and pecans, and mix well. Pour into a 2-quart baking dish that has been prepared with nonstick cooking spray.

Bake 30–35 minutes or until a knife inserted in the center comes out clean. Makes 6 servings.

# MASHED POTATO NESTS

| | |
|---:|:---|
| 1½ cups | **leftover mashed potatoes** |
| 6 | **eggs** |
| 2 cups | **grated cheddar cheese** |
| ½ cup | **milk** |
| 1 teaspoon | **Worcestershire sauce** |
| 1 teaspoon | **prepared mustard** |
| ¼ teaspoon | **salt** |
| ¼ teaspoon | **pepper** |

Preheat oven on broil and place cooking rack 6 inches from heat. Prepare 6 small souffle dishes generously with nonstick cooking spray.

Line dishes with mashed potatoes, pressing up sides. Break 1 egg into each cup. Broil for 5–7 minutes until eggs are set.

In a saucepan, blend cheese and milk, cook over medium until hot but not boiling. Add Worcestershire sauce, mustard, salt, and pepper and mix well. Pour evenly over each cup. Place in broiler and cook until cheese is lightly browned. About 3 minutes. Gently remove from dishes and place on serving plates. Makes 6 servings.

# BURRITOS, SANDWICHES, & WRAPS

# BREAKFAST BURRITOS

| | |
|---:|:---|
| 1 package (30 ounces) | **shredded hash brown potatoes** |
| 1 pound | **country sausage** |
| 24 | **eggs** |
| 1 cup | **milk** |
| 1½ teaspoon | **Mrs. Dash** |
| 1½ teaspoon | **salt** |
| 24 (8-inch) | **flour tortillas** |
| 2 cups | **grated cheddar cheese** |
| 1 can (5 ounces) | **diced green chiles** |

Preheat oven to 375 degrees.

Prepare hash browns according to package directions and brown sausage in a large frying pan. Drain.

In a large bowl, mix eggs, milk, and seasonings. Heat a large frying pan over medium heat and pour mixture in pan. As eggs begin to set, gently pull the eggs across the pan with an inverted turner, forming large soft curds. Continue cooking—pulling, lifting, and folding eggs—until thickened and no visible liquid egg remains. Do not stir constantly.

In each flour tortilla, place 2 tablespoons of sausage, 2 tablespoons hash browns and 2 tablespoons of the egg mixture. Sprinkle with cheese and green chiles.

Roll tortilla into a burrito and wrap in aluminum foil. Place burritos on baking sheet and bake for 10 minutes. Serve with salsa and sour cream if desired. Makes 24 servings.

# GREEN CHILE BURRITOS

| | |
|---:|:---|
| 1 package (30 ounces) | **shredded hash brown potatoes** |
| 1 | **green or red bell pepper,** chopped |
| ½ | **onion,** finely chopped |
| 1 tablespoon | **butter or margarine** |
| 6 | **eggs,** beaten |
| 6 (8-inch) | **flour tortillas** |
| 2 cans (4 ounces each) | **whole green chiles** |
| 2 cups | **grated cheddar cheese,** divided |
| 1 can (15 ounces) | **green chile sauce,** warmed |

In a large frying pan, saute hash browns, bell pepper, and onion in butter. Add eggs and stir until set. Warm tortillas on the stove or in the microwave.

Slice green chiles in half, clean out seeds, and place one on each tortilla. Add egg mixture along with a sprinkle of cheese. Roll tortilla up and place seam side down on a plate. Spoon sauce over burrito. Makes 4–6 servings.

# BREAKFAST BRUSCHETTA

| | |
|---:|:---|
| 1 can (14.5 ounces) | **diced canned tomatoes,** drained |
| 2 tablespoons | **olive oil** |
| 2 teaspoons | **minced garlic** |
| 1 tablespoon | **dried basil** |
| 1/4 teaspoon | **salt** |
| 1/8 teaspoon | **pepper** |
| 1 | **French bread baguette,** sliced into 12 diagonal pieces and lightly toasted |
| 1/4 cup | **grated mozzarella cheese** |
| 1/2 cup | **grated fresh Parmesan cheese** |
| 4 | **eggs** |
| 2 tablespoons | **milk** |

Place tomatoes, oil, garlic, basil, salt, and pepper in a medium bowl. Mix well and allow to sit for 30 minutes, or place in refrigerator overnight for flavors to blend.

Preheat oven to 350 degrees.

Arrange baguette slices on large baking sheet. Sprinkle cheeses on top and bake for 2–4 minutes or until cheeses are melted.

Meanwhile, whisk together eggs and milk in small bowl. Prepare a large frying pan with nonstick cooking spray and place over medium-high heat. Pour mixture into pan and as eggs begin to set, gently pull the eggs across the pan with an inverted turner, forming large soft curds. Continue cooking—pulling, lifting, and folding eggs—until thickened and no visible liquid egg remains. Do not stir constantly. Spoon on top of baguette slices and top with tomato mixture. Makes 6 servings.

# EGG SALAD SANDWICH

| | |
|---:|:---|
| 6 | **hard-boiled eggs,** chopped |
| 2 tablespoons | **mayonnaise** |
| 1 tablespoon | **mustard** |
| 1/3 cup | **pickle relish** |
| 1 teaspoon | **salt** |
| 1/4 teaspoon | **pepper** |
| 12 slices | **bread** |

In a medium bowl, combine eggs, mayonnaise, mustard, pickle relish, salt, and pepper. Mix well. Spread the mixture on 6 slices of bread. Top with remaining slices. Makes 6 servings.

# BAGEL SANDWICH

|  |  |
|---:|:---|
| 3 | **mushrooms** |
| 2 teaspoons | **butter or margarine** |
| dash | **Italian seasonings** |
| 1 | **plain bagel,** sliced in half |
| 4 | **eggs** |
| 4 tablespoons | **half-and-half** |
| 1/2 cup | **grated cheddar cheese,** divided |

Slice the mushrooms and saute in butter until lightly browned; sprinkle with Italian seasonings. Keep warm. Lightly toast the bagel slices.

In a small bowl, combine eggs with half-and-half. Prepare a large frying pan with nonstick cooking spray and place over medium-high heat. Pour mixture into pan and as eggs begin to set, gently pull the eggs across the pan with an inverted turner, forming large soft curds. Continue cooking—pulling, lifting, and folding eggs—until thickened and no visible liquid egg remains.

Place a bagel slice onto separate plates. Using a spatula, transfer half the eggs onto each bagel. Top with half of the cheese and half of the mushrooms. Makes 2 servings.

# MONSTER SUB

| | |
|---:|:---|
| 1 | **unsliced loaf French bread** |
| 4 tablespoons | **butter or margarine,** divided |
| 2 tablespoons | **mayonnaise** |
| 4 thin slices | **deli ham** |
| 4 thin slices | **deli turkey** |
| 4 strips | **fried bacon** |
| 1 | **large tomato,** sliced |
| 1 | **small onion,** thinly sliced |
| 2 tablespoons | **honey mustard** |
| 8 | **eggs,** lightly beaten |
| 4 slices | **cheddar cheese** |
| 4 slices | **pepper jack cheese** |

Preheat oven to 375 degrees.

Cut bread in half lengthwise; carefully hollow out top and bottom, leaving $1/2$-inch shells. Spread 3 tablespoons of butter and all of the mayonnaise inside bread shells. Line bottom bread shell with ham, turkey, and bacon. Top with tomato, onion, and honey mustard.

In a frying pan, melt remaining butter; add eggs. Cook over medium heat, stirring occasionally until eggs are almost set. Spoon into bottom bread shell on top of meats and top with cheeses. Cover with bread top. Wrap in aluminum foil that has been lightly prepared with nonstick cooking spray. Bake for 15–20 minutes or until heated through. Cut and serve. Makes 6–8 servings.

# EGGS IN A NEST

| | |
|--:|:--|
| 2 slices | **toast** |
| | **butter or margarine,** to taste |
| 2 tablespoons | **grated cheddar cheese,** divided |
| 2 | **eggs** |
| | **salt and pepper,** to taste |
| 2 strips | **bacon,** cooked and crumbled |

Preheat oven to 350 degrees. Spread toast with butter and half of cheese.

Separate eggs and place whites in a mixing bowl and leave yolks in shell until needed. Season with salt and pepper and beat until stiff, but still fluffy. Gently fold in bacon.

Place toast on a baking sheet and evenly divide the egg white mixture in heaps onto toast slices. Make a dent in centers and place the yolks in the nests. Sprinkle with remaining cheese.

Bake until cheese is browned and egg is set. Makes 2 servings.

# MEXI EGGS-IN-A-HOLE

| | |
|---:|:---|
| 2 tablespoons | **butter or margarine,** room temperature |
| 4 slices | **sourdough bread** |
| 4 | **eggs** |
| ¼ cup | **grated pepper jack cheese,** divided |
| ¼ cup | **salsa** |

Preheat oven to broil.

Spread butter evenly on both sides of bread slices. Cut a 2–3 inch circle from center of each slice.

Warm a large nonstick frying pan with an ovenproof handle over medium heat. Place 2 bread slices in pan and break 1 egg into center of each slice. Cook until bottoms of eggs are set, 2–3 minutes; gently turn over. Cook until egg whites are completely set and yolks begin to thicken but are not hard.

Sprinkle 1 tablespoon cheese onto each bread slice. Broil 4 inches from heat just until cheese is melted, about 1 minute. Repeat to cook remaining eggs. Serve with salsa. Makes 4 servings.

# STUFFED ROLL

| | |
|---:|:---|
| 1 | **large French roll** |
| | **salt and pepper,** to taste |
| 2 | **eggs,** beaten |
| 2 tablespoons | **grated sharp cheddar cheese** |
| 2 slices | **bacon,** cooked crisp and crumbled |
| | **paprika** |

Preheat oven to 375 degrees.

Cut a lid off the roll and remove soft bread, leaving a shell. Add salt and pepper to eggs and pour into roll. Add cheese, then bacon. Sprinkle with paprika. Place on baking sheet and bake until egg is set and roll is crisp, about 15 minutes. Makes 1 serving.

# HAM AND CHEESE ROLLS

| | |
|--:|:--|
| 3 slices | **bacon** |
| 1 cup | **sliced mushrooms** |
| ½ cup | **chopped onion** |
| ½ cup | **chopped green bell pepper** |
| 6 | **eggs** |
| ¼ cup | **milk** |
| 6 | **bread rolls** |
| 6 thin slices | **ham** |
| 6 thin slices | **tomato** |
| 6 thin slices | **Swiss cheese** |

Preheat oven to broil.

Cook bacon in large nonstick frying pan over medium heat until crisp; drain and crumble. Add mushrooms, onion, and bell pepper to pan; saute until tender, about 5 minutes. Add bacon to the vegetables.

Beat eggs and milk in medium bowl until blended. Pour over mixture in pan, stirring occasionally to mix in uncooked eggs, and cook until done.

Split rolls in half. Pinch out middle of the bottom half. Spoon egg mixture onto holes, dividing evenly. Top each with 1 slice of ham, tomato, and cheese. Broil 6 inches from heat until cheese is melted, about 3 minutes. Cover with roll tops. Makes 6 servings.

# ORIENTAL WRAPS

| | |
|---:|:---|
| 6 | **eggs** |
| 4 strips | **bacon,** cooked and crumbled |
| 2 tablespoons | **finely chopped water chestnuts** |
| 1 | **finely sliced green onion** |
| 6 tablespoons | **milk** |
| 1/4 cup | **soy sauce** |
| 1 tablespoon | **sesame oil** |
| 1 tablespoon | **rice wine vinegar** |
| 1/2 teaspoon | **grated orange peel** |
| 1/2 teaspoon | **grated ginger root** |
| 1 clove | **garlic,** crushed |

Beat together the eggs, bacon, water chestnuts, onion, and milk. Pour half into an 8-inch round glass microwave-safe baking dish that has been prepared with nonstick cooking spray. Microwave on high until the egg sheet is firm and dry, about 2 minutes. Let cool. Remove the egg sheet from the dish and roll up. Repeat with the rest of the egg mixture.

Combine the soy sauce, sesame oil, vinegar, orange peel, ginger, and garlic in a small bowl and mix thoroughly. Serve as a dipping sauce for the wraps. Makes 2 servings.

# SOUTHWESTERN EGG WRAPS

| | |
|---:|:---|
| 6 | **large tortillas** |
| 1 can (15 ounces) | **refried beans** |
| 1 cup | **salsa** |
| 1 cup | **grated cheddar cheese** |
| 6 | **hard-boiled eggs,** chopped |
| 1 can (4.25 ounces) | **chopped black olives** |
| ¾ cup | **chopped green onions** |
| ¾ cup | **chopped tomato** |

Preheat a non-stick griddle to medium temperature. Toast tortillas on one side.

With grilled side down, spread each tortilla with refried beans. Top evenly with salsa, cheese, egg, olives, onion, and tomato. Roll each tortilla tightly around ingredients and place, 3 at a time, on a large microwave safe plate. Microwave 1 minute on high. Let stand for 2 minutes. Makes 6 servings.

# QUICHES & SOUFFLES

# HASH BROWN QUICHE

| | |
|---:|:---|
| 1 package (30 ounces) | **frozen shredded hash brown potatoes,** thawed |
| 1 tablespoon | **butter or margarine** |
| 1 | **small onion,** chopped |
| 2 teaspoons | **minced garlic** |
| 1 | **small zucchini,** diced |
| 1 | **small red bell pepper,** diced |
| 1 | **small yellow squash,** diced |
| 4 | **eggs** |
| 1/2 cup | **milk** |
| 1/2 cup | **grated mozzarella cheese** |
| 1/2 teaspoon | **basil** |
| 1/2 teaspoon | **oregano** |

Preheat oven to 425 degrees.

Press hash browns evenly on bottom and sides of 10-inch quiche dish or pie plate that has been prepared with nonstick cooking spray. Coat hash browns lightly with cooking spray. Bake until lightly browned and crisp, about 30 minutes. Reduce oven setting to 375 degrees.

Heat butter in large nonstick frying pan over medium heat until melted. Add onion and garlic; saute until tender. Add zucchini, bell pepper, and squash; saute until tender.

Beat eggs, milk, cheese, basil, and oregano in large bowl. Add vegetables and toss to mix. Pour mixture into hash brown crust and bake 45–50 minutes or until knife inserted near center comes out clean. Let stand 5 minutes before serving. Makes 4 servings.

# ITALIAN QUICHE

| | |
|---:|:---|
| ¼ cup | **chopped green bell pepper** |
| ¼ cup | **chopped red bell pepper** |
| ¼ cup | **chopped onion** |
| 1 tablespoon | **olive oil** |
| 1 teaspoon | **minced garlic** |
| 1 cup | **grated mozzarella cheese** |
| 2 tablespoons | **pesto** |
| 1 (9-inch) | **refrigerated piecrust** |
| 6 strips | **bacon,** cooked and crumbled |
| ¼ cup | **chopped sun-dried tomatoes** |
| 6 | **eggs** |
| ¾ cup | **milk** |
| 1 cup | **finely crushed croutons** |

Preheat oven to 350 degrees.

In a small frying pan, saute bell peppers and onion in oil until tender and onion is slightly translucent. Remove vegetables from pan and set aside. Saute garlic in same pan until lightly browned; set aside.

Toss mozzarella with pesto until evenly distributed. Place the piecrust in a glass 9-inch pie pan. In layers, add bacon, mozzarella mix, cooked vegetables, and tomatoes.

In a medium bowl, beat eggs and milk. Mix in garlic and pour over the bacon and vegetables. Sprinkle the croutons over the top. Bake for 40–45 minutes or until a knife inserted in the center comes out clean. Makes 6 servings.

# SPINACH AND ASIAGO QUICHE

| | |
|---:|:---|
| 4 | **eggs,** divided |
| 2 cups | **frozen shredded hash brown potatoes,** thawed |
| 1/4 cup | **grated Asiago cheese** |
| 1/4 cup | **frozen chopped spinach,** thawed |
| 1 tablespoon | **chopped chives** |
| 1 strip | **bacon,** cooked and crumbled |
| 1/3 cup | **grated Colby Jack cheese** |
| | **salt and pepper,** to taste |

Preheat oven to 350 degrees. Prepare a 12-cup muffin pan with nonstick cooking spray.*

Mix one egg, hash browns, and Asiago cheese in a bowl. Divide mixture evenly between 8 muffin cups. Press mixture evenly on bottom and sides of cups. Bake until hash browns are lightly browned, about 7 minutes.

In a medium bowl, beat remaining eggs. Add spinach, chives, bacon, Colby Jack cheese, salt, and pepper; toss to mix. Put 2 tablespoons of the egg mixture into the center of each cup. Return to oven for 15 minutes or until a toothpick inserted in the center comes out clean. Makes 8 servings.

*Tip: Fill the empty cups half full with water before baking. This will prevent damage to your pan.

# SALMON QUICHE

| | |
|--:|:--|
| 1 (9-inch) | **refrigerated piecrust** |
| 1 pound | **salmon,** cooked and flaked |
| 2 cups | **chopped asparagus** |
| 1 1/2 cups | **grated Swiss cheese** |
| 6 | **eggs** |
| 1/2 cup | **milk** |
| 1 teaspoon | **dill** |
| | **salt and pepper,** to taste |

Preheat oven to 400 degrees.

Place the pie crust in a 9-inch glass pie pan. In layers, add the salmon, asparagus, and cheese.

In a medium bowl, beat the eggs and combine with milk, dill, salt, and pepper. Pour the egg mixture over the cheese and bake for 40–45 minutes or until a knife inserted in the center comes out clean. Makes 8 servings.

# SEAFOOD SOUFFLE

| | |
|---:|:---|
| 4 tablespoons | **salted butter or margarine** |
| ¼ cup | **finely chopped celery** |
| 1 teaspoon | **minced garlic** |
| ½ teaspoon | **curry powder** |
| ½ teaspoon | **dried thyme** |
| ½ teaspoon | **red pepper flakes** |
| 3 tablespoons | **flour** |
| ¾ cup | **milk** |
| ½ cup | **half-and-half** |
| ½ cup | **sweetened flaked coconut** |
| 6 | **eggs,** separated |
| ½ pound | **crabmeat** |
| ½ | **lemon,** juiced |

Preheat oven to 400 degrees. Prepare 8 ramekins with nonstick cooking spray.

In a medium frying pan, melt butter over low heat and saute celery, garlic, curry powder, thyme, and red pepper flakes for 3 minutes. Stir in flour until smooth, about 1 minute. Pour in milk and half-and-half and increase heat to medium, stirring constantly, until mixture comes to a boil and thickens. Set aside to cool.

Toast coconut in a small frying pan over low heat until lightly golden. Set aside. In a large bowl, beat 4 egg yolks until thick and lemon colored. Once sauce has cooled, add to egg yolks and mix well. Add coconut and crab meat and mix.

In medium bowl, beat 6 egg whites and lemon juice until stiff peaks form. Gradually fold crab mixture into egg whites and lightly mix. Spoon into ramekins and place in a baking pan. Fill the pan half full with hot water. Bake for 25–30 minutes or until puffy and delicately brown. Makes 8 servings.

# CHEESE SOUFFLE

| | |
|---:|:---|
| 1 cup | **cottage cheese** |
| ½ cup | **mayonnaise** |
| 2 teaspoons | **Dijon mustard** |
| 1 cup | **grated sharp cheddar cheese** |
| 4 | **eggs,** separated and at room temperature |
| ½ teaspoon | **cream of tartar** |

Preheat oven to 350 degrees.

In a large bowl, mix cottage cheese, mayonnaise, and mustard until creamy. Add cheese and combine. In another bowl, beat the egg yolks until thick and lemon colored. Fold yolks into cheese mixture until well combined.

In medium bowl, beat egg whites and cream of tartar until stiff peaks form. Gradually fold cheese mixture into the egg whites and lightly mix until well blended. Pour into a 2-quart souffle dish that has been prepared with nonstick cooking spray and bake for 45–50 minutes or until puffy and delicately brown. Makes 6 servings.

# PUMPKIN SOUFFLE

|  |  |
|---:|:---|
|  | **powdered sugar** |
| 6 | **eggs,** separated and room temperature |
| ¾ teaspoon | **cream of tartar** |
| ½ cup | **sugar** |
| ½ cup | **canned spiced pumpkin** |

Preheat oven to 375 degrees. Prepare 6 ramekins with nonstick cooking spray. Coat with powdered sugar and set aside.

In large bowl, beat egg whites and cream of tartar until foamy. Add the sugar by tablespoons until it has completely dissolved and the eggs become glossy and form soft peaks. Set aside.

In another bowl, beat the egg yolks until thick and lemon colored. Fold pumpkin into egg yolks until thoroughly mixed. Gradually fold pumpkin mixture into the egg whites and lightly mix until well blended. Spoon into ramekins.

Place the ramekins in a baking pan and fill the pan half full with hot water. Bake for 15–20 minutes or until puffy and delicately brown. Sprinkle with powdered sugar and serve. Makes 6 servings.

# CHEESY LAYERED SOUFFLE

| | |
|---:|:---|
| 14 | **egg whites,** room temperature |
| 1 teaspoon | **cream of tartar** |
| 3 | **egg yolks** |
| ¾ cup | **milk,** divided |
| 1 cup | **grated cheddar cheese** |
| 1 can (2 ounces) | **diced mild green chiles** |
| ½ cup | **Velveeta cheese** |
| 6 strips | **bacon,** cooked and crumbled |

Preheat oven to 350 degrees. In medium bowl, beat egg whites and cream of tartar until stiff peaks begin to form.

In another bowl, beat the egg yolks until thick and lemon colored. Fold in ½ cup milk and cheddar cheese. Gradually fold cheese mixture into the egg whites and lightly mix until well blended. Pour into two 9-inch round cake pans that have been prepared with nonstick cooking spray and bake for 20–30 minutes or until puffy and delicately brown.

In a microwave safe bowl, combine remaining milk, chiles, and Velveeta and heat in the microwave on high for 30 seconds. Remove and stir. Repeat until mixture is smooth.

Invert one souffle onto a platter, top with ⅓ of the chile mixture and sprinkle with ⅓ of the bacon. Place the second souffle, face up, on top and drizzle with remaining chile mixture and bacon. Makes 10–12 servings.

# RASPBERRY BLINTZ SOUFFLE

| | |
|---:|:---|
| 8 | **eggs,** separated and room temperature |
| ¾ teaspoon | **cream of tartar** |
| 1½ cups | **sour cream** |
| ½ cup | **orange juice** |
| ¼ cup | **butter or margarine,** softened |
| 1 cup | **flour** |
| ⅓ cup | **sugar** |
| 2 teaspoons | **baking powder** |
| ½ teaspoon | **cinnamon** |
| 16 ounces | **cottage cheese** |
| 1 tablespoon | **sugar** |
| 1 teaspoon | **vanilla** |
| 8 ounces | **cream cheese,** softened |
| 1 cup | **raspberries** |

In a large bowl, beat egg whites and cream of tartar until stiff peaks begin to form. In a blender, combine sour cream, juice, 6 egg yolks, butter, flour, ⅓ cup sugar, baking powder, and cinnamon. Blend well, scraping sides occasionally. Gradually fold sour cream mixture into the egg whites and lightly mix until well blended.

In a large bowl, mix cottage cheese, 1 tablespoon sugar, vanilla, and cream cheese. In another bowl, beat remaining egg yolks until thick and lemon colored; fold into cheese until well mixed. Pour half of the egg white mixture into a 9 x 13-inch glass baking dish that has been prepared with nonstick cooking spray. Drop cheese mixture by spoonfuls over the batter. Spread evenly and top with raspberries. Pour remaining egg white mixture over top and spread evenly. Cover and refrigerate overnight.

Preheat oven to 350 degrees. Bake 50–65 minutes or until puffy and delicately brown. Makes 10–12 servings.

# BAKED, STRATTAS, & CASSEROLES

# EGG PUFF BRUNCH

| | |
|---:|:---|
| 8 slices | **white bread,** cubed |
| 2 cups | **grated sharp cheddar cheese** |
| 6 | **eggs** |
| 2 cups | **milk** |
| 1 teaspoon | **dry mustard** |
| | **salt and pepper,** to taste |

Place the bread in single layer in a 9 x 13-inch baking dish that has been prepared with nonstick cooking spray. Top with cheese.

Beat eggs, milk, mustard, salt, and pepper in medium bowl until blended. Slowly pour over bread and cheese in baking dish. Cover and refrigerate several hours or overnight.

Preheat oven to 350 degrees.

Remove from refrigerator; uncover and let stand while oven heats. Bake in center of oven until puffed, golden, and knife inserted near center comes out clean, 50–60 minutes. Let it set 5–10 minutes before serving. Makes 6–8 servings.

# MEXICAN-STYLE EGGS-IN-A-NEST

| | |
|---:|:---|
| 2 cups | **shredded hash brown potatoes** |
| 1 cup | **grated Mexican-blend cheese** |
| 1/2 teaspoon | **taco seasoning** |
| 4 | **eggs** |
| | **salt and pepper,** to taste |

Preheat oven to 375 degrees.

In a medium bowl, combine hash browns, cheese, and taco seasoning and mix until seasoning is evenly distributed.

Divide mixture evenly among 4 ramekins prepared with nonstick cooking spray. Form a crust along the bottoms and halfway up sides. Place on baking sheet and bake for 10 minutes.

Remove from oven and crack one egg into each nest. Bake until whites are completely set and yolks are as desired, 10–15 minutes longer. Sprinkle with salt and pepper. Makes 4 servings.

# HAWAIIAN ENCHILADAS

| | |
|---:|:---|
| ½ cup | **thinly sliced carrots** |
| ½ cup | **thinly sliced celery** |
| 1 can (15 ounces) | **pineapple chunks,** drained |
| ½ cup | **dried apricots,** chopped |
| 1 | **chicken breast,** cooked and diced |
| 1 cup | **sweet and sour sauce** |
| ½ cup | **slivered almonds** |
| 2 cups | **grated Monterey Jack cheese** |
| 8 (8-inch) | **flour tortillas** |
| 2 tablespoons | **flour** |
| 1 teaspoon | **ground mustard** |
| ½ teaspoon | **salt** |
| 2 cups | **milk,** divided |
| 6 | **eggs,** beaten |

Steam carrots and celery until crisp-tender. In a medium bowl, combine pineapple, carrots, celery, apricots, chicken, sweet and sour sauce, almonds, and cheese; toss to mix. Spoon filling equally among tortillas. Tightly roll up each tortilla and place, seam side down, in a 9 x 13-inch baking dish that has been generously prepared with nonstick cooking spray.

In a medium bowl, combine flour, mustard, salt, and 3 tablespoons milk; stir until smooth. Add eggs and remaining milk and mix thoroughly. Pour over tortillas. Cover and refrigerate several hours or overnight.

Preheat oven to 350 degrees.

Remove from refrigerator; uncover and let stand while oven heats. Bake in center of oven until puffed, golden, and knife inserted near center comes out clean, 40–50 minutes. Makes 8 servings.

# ARTICHOKE EGG BAKE

|   |   |
|--:|:--|
| 8 | **eggs** |
| 1 cup | **sour cream** |
| 2 teaspoons | **Mrs. Dash** |
| 1 can (15 ounces) | **artichoke hearts,** drained |
| 1 cup | **grated Colby Jack cheese** |
| 1 can (4 ounces) | **mushrooms,** drained |

Preheat oven to 350 degrees.

In a medium bowl, beat eggs; add sour cream and Mrs. Dash and mix well. Add artichokes, cheese, and mushrooms and thoroughly combine. Pour into an 8 x 8-inch baking dish that has been prepared with nonstick cooking spray.

Bake in center of oven until puffed, golden, and knife inserted near center comes out clean, 25–30 minutes. Makes 6 servings.

# BROCCOLI AND EGG BAKE

| | |
|---:|:---|
| 2 cups | **frozen chopped broccoli,** steamed and well drained |
| 1 can (4 ounces) | **sliced mushrooms** |
| 2 tablespoons | **salted butter or margarine,** melted |
| 8 | **hard-boiled eggs,** sliced |
| 1 can (10.75 ounces) | **cream of mushroom soup,** condensed |
| 2 tablespoons | **mayonnaise** |
| 1 tablespoon | **lime juice** |
| | **salt and pepper,** to taste |
| 1 teaspoon | **curry powder** |
| 1 cup | **grated mozzarella cheese** |

Preheat oven to 350 degrees. In a medium bowl, combine broccoli, mushrooms, and butter. Toss to mix.

Lightly prepare a 9 x 11-inch glass baking dish with nonstick cooking spray. Pour in broccoli mixture and distribute evenly in dish. Layer the eggs over the broccoli.

In a medium bowl, combine the soup, mayonnaise, lime juice, salt, pepper, and curry powder. Pour mixture evenly over the eggs. Bake for 20–25 minutes. Sprinkle cheese over the top and return to the oven for 5 minutes or until cheese is melted and becomes lightly browned. Makes 6–8 servings.

# SPINACH-HASH BROWN POCKETS

| | |
|---:|:---|
| 2 tablespoons | **butter or margarine** |
| 2 cups | **shredded hash brown potatoes** |
| 1/4 cup | **diced red bell pepper** |
| 1/4 cup | **diced yellow onion** |
| 1 cup | **frozen spinach,** thawed and drained |
| 1/2 cup | **sour cream** |
| 1/2 cup | **grated cheddar cheese,** divided |
| 1 teaspoon | **dried dill weed** |
| 4 | **eggs** |

Preheat oven to 350 degrees.

In a large nonstick frying pan over medium-high heat, melt butter. Add hash browns, bell pepper, and onion and cook until hash browns begin to crisp and onion becomes limp. Remove from heat and add spinach, sour cream, 1/4 cup cheese, and dill weed; mix thoroughly.

Divide mixture evenly among 4 ramekins that have been prepared with nonstick cooking spray. Form a pocket in the center, about 2 inches in diameter. Place ramekins on baking sheet and bake for 10 minutes.

Remove from oven and crack one egg into each pocket and top with remaining cheese. Bake until whites are completely set and yolks are as desired, 10–15 minutes longer. Sprinkle with salt and pepper. Makes 4 servings.

# BENEDICT STRATA

| | |
|---:|:---|
| 1 package (12 ounces) | **English muffins** |
| 6 slices | **Canadian bacon,** chopped |
| 6 | **eggs** |
| 1½ cups | **milk** |
| 2 tablespoons | **mayonnaise** |
| 2 tablespoons | **fresh lemon juice** |
| 2 teaspoons | **freshly grated lemon peel** |

Split muffins and cut into 1-inch pieces. Place half of the pieces in single layer in an 8-inch square baking dish that has been prepared with nonstick cooking spray. Top with half of the bacon. Repeat layers with remaining muffin pieces and bacon.

Beat eggs, milk, mayonnaise, lemon juice, and lemon peel in medium bowl until blended. Slowly pour over layers in baking dish. Cover and refrigerate several hours or overnight.

Preheat oven to 350 degrees.

Remove strata from refrigerator; uncover and let stand while oven heats. Bake in center of oven until puffed, golden, and knife inserted near center comes out clean, 50–60 minutes. Let it set 5–10 minutes before serving. Makes 6 servings.

# HAM AND CHEESE STRATA

| | |
|---:|:---|
| 6 slices | **French bread,** cubed |
| 1 cup | **diced ham** |
| 1 cup | **grated cheddar cheese,** divided |
| 6 | **eggs** |
| 2 cups | **half-and-half** |
| 1/2 teaspoon | **dry mustard** |
| | **salt and pepper,** to taste |
| 1/2 cup | **sliced green onions** |

Place half of the bread cubes in bottom of a 9 x 13-inch glass baking dish that has been prepared with nonstick cooking spray. Evenly distribute the ham and 1/2 cup cheese over bread. Top with remaining bread.

In a medium bowl, beat eggs, half-and-half, mustard, salt, and pepper. Pour over bread. Spread remaining cheese on top. Cover and refrigerate overnight.

Preheat oven to 375 degrees.

Remove strata from refrigerator; uncover and let stand while oven heats. Bake in center of oven until puffed, golden, and knife inserted near center comes out clean, 45–50 minutes. Let it set 5–10 minutes before serving. Makes 6–8 servings.

# SAUSAGE AND PEPPERONI STRATA

| | |
|---:|:---|
| ½ pound | **ground sausage** |
| 1 package (3.5 ounces) | **pepperoni,** diced |
| 1 | **large zucchini,** diced |
| 1 can (14.75 ounces) | **creamed corn** |
| ½ cup | **diced roasted red bell pepper** |
| 1 tablespoon | **chopped garlic** |
| 1 teaspoon each | **basil, parsley, and sage** |
| 1 cup | **grated Swiss cheese,** divided |
| 1 cup | **grated cheddar cheese,** divided |
| 6 slices | **Italian bread,** cubed |
| 5 | **eggs** |
| 2 cups | **half-and-half** |
| 1 teaspoon | **salt** |
| ¼ teaspoon | **pepper** |

In a 12-inch frying pan, cook sausage until it begins to brown. Add the pepperoni, zucchini, corn, bell pepper, garlic, basil, parsley, and sage. Cook 2–5 minutes until zucchini is tender. Combine cheeses in a bowl.

Place half of the bread cubes in bottom of an 11 x 13-inch glass baking dish that has been prepared with nonstick cooking spray. Evenly layer half the sausage mixture and 1 cup of cheese over bread. Top with remaining bread and remaining sausage mixture. In a medium bowl, beat eggs, half-and-half, salt, and pepper. Pour over bread. Spread remaining cheese on top. Cover and refrigerate overnight.

Preheat oven to 350 degrees. Remove strata from refrigerator; uncover and let stand while oven heats. Bake in center of oven until puffed, golden, and knife inserted near center comes out clean, 35–45 minutes. Let it set 5–10 minutes before serving. Makes 8–10 servings.

# SEAFOOD STRATA

| | |
|---:|:---|
| 1/2 cup | **slivered red onion** |
| 1 cup | **diced celery** |
| 1/4 cup | **diced yellow bell pepper** |
| 1/4 cup | **diced green bell pepper** |
| 1/4 cup | **diced red bell pepper** |
| 2 1/2 cups | **grated Swiss cheese,** divided |
| 1 pound | **deli-style seafood salad** |
| 6 slices | **French bread,** cubed |
| 5 | **eggs** |
| 2 cups | **milk** |
| 1 cup | **half-and-half** |
| 1/4 teaspoon | **dried mustard** |
| | **salt and pepper,** to taste |

In a large bowl combine onion, celery, bell peppers, 1 1/2 cups cheese, and seafood salad. Toss to mix.

Place half of the bread cubes in bottom of a 9 x 13-inch glass baking dish that has been prepared with nonstick cooking spray. Evenly layer half the seafood mixture over bread. Top with another layer of the remaining bread and remaining seafood mixture.

In a medium bowl, beat eggs, milk, half-and-half, and mustard. Pour over bread. Spread remaining cheese on top. Cover and refrigerate overnight.

Preheat oven to 350 degrees. Remove strata from refrigerator; uncover and let stand while oven heats. Bake in center of oven until puffed, golden, and knife inserted near center comes out clean, 45–50 minutes. Let it set 5–10 minutes before serving. Makes 6–8 servings.

# STRATA MILANO

| | |
|---:|:---|
| 5 | **eggs** |
| 2 cups | **milk** |
| ½ cup | **half-and-half** |
| 1 teaspoon | **salt** |
| ½ teaspoon | **cayenne pepper** |
| 6 slices | **bacon,** cooked and crumbled |
| 1 cup | **ricotta cheese** |
| ½ cup | **crumbled feta cheese** |
| 1 can (15 ounces) | **diced tomatoes,** with liquid |
| 1 cup | **chopped red onion** |
| 1½ teaspoon | **dried rosemary** |
| 1 loaf (16 ounces) | **sourdough bread,** cubed |

In a large bowl, beat eggs, milk, half-and-half, salt, and cayenne pepper. Add bacon, cheeses, tomatoes, onion, and rosemary and mix well.

Place half of the bread cubes in bottom of a 9 x 13-inch glass baking dish that has been prepared with nonstick cooking spray. Evenly layer half the tomato and egg mixture over bread. Top with remaining bread and remaining tomato and egg mixture. Cover and refrigerate overnight.

Preheat oven to 350 degrees.

Remove strata from refrigerator; uncover and let stand while oven heats. Bake in center of oven until puffed, golden, and knife inserted near center comes out clean, 50–60 minutes. Let it set 5–10 minutes before serving. Makes 6–8 servings.

# SPINACH AND CHEESE CROISSANT STRATA

| | |
|---:|:---|
| 8 | **large croissants,** cubed |
| 2 cups | **grated Monterey Jack cheese,** divided |
| 1 package (10 ounces) | **cut frozen spinach,** thawed and drained |
| 8 | **eggs** |
| 1 cup | **milk** |
| 1 cup | **half-and-half** |
| dash | **Worcestershire sauce** |
| 1 teaspoon | **basil** |

Layer croissant cubes in bottom of a 9 x 13-inch glass baking dish that has been prepared with nonstick cooking spray. Evenly layer 1 cup of cheese over bread and top with spinach.

In a medium bowl, beat eggs, milk, half-and-half, Worcestershire sauce, and basil. Pour over bread. Spread remaining cheese on top. Cover and refrigerate overnight.

Preheat oven to 350 degrees.

Remove strata from refrigerator; uncover and let stand while oven heats. Bake in center of oven until puffed, golden, and knife inserted near center comes out clean, 50–60 minutes. Let it set 5–10 minutes before serving. Makes 6–8 servings.

# CHILI EGG PUFF

| | |
|---:|:---|
| 5 | **eggs** |
| ¼ cup | **flour** |
| ½ teaspoon | **baking powder** |
| ¼ teaspoon | **salt** |
| ¼ pound | **sharp cheddar cheese,** cubed |
| ½ pound | **pepper jack cheese,** cubed |
| 1 container (8 ounces) | **cottage cheese** |
| 1 can (4 ounces) | **diced green chiles** |
| ¼ cup | **butter or margarine,** melted |

Preheat oven to 375 degrees.

In a medium bowl, beat eggs. Add flour, baking powder, and salt; stir until smooth. Mix in cheeses, chiles, and butter. Pour into a 9 x 11-inch baking pan that has been prepared with nonstick cooking spray and bake in center of oven until puffed, golden, and knife inserted near center comes out clean, 25–30 minutes. Makes 6 servings.

# QUICK EGG CASSEROLE

| | |
|---:|:---|
| 2 dozen | **eggs** |
| 1 can (10.75 ounces) | **cream of mushroom soup,** condensed |
| 1 cup | **milk** |
| 2 cups | **grated cheddar cheese,** divided |
| 1 pound | **bacon,** cooked and crumbled |
| 2 tablespoons | **Mrs. Dash** |

Preheat oven to 350 degrees.

In a large bowl, beat eggs. Add soup and milk. Mix in 1½ cups cheese and bacon. Pour into a 9 x 13-inch baking dish that has been prepared with nonstick cooking spray and top with remaining cheese. Bake in center of oven until puffed, golden, and knife inserted near center comes out clean, 35–40 minutes. Makes 12 servings.

# EGG LASAGNA

| | |
|---:|:---|
| 12 | **eggs** |
| 1 package (8 ounces) | **cream cheese,** softened |
| 2 tablespoons | **butter or margarine** |
| ½ cup | **diced red bell pepper** |
| ¼ cup | **diced onion** |
| ½ cup | **diced zucchini** |
| 8 | **medium mushrooms,** diced |
| 1 pound | **ground sausage** |
| 12 slices | **bacon,** cooked and crumbled |
| ½ cup | **grated pepper jack cheese** |
| ½ cup | **grated cheddar cheese** |

Preheat oven to 350 degrees.

In a medium bowl, beat eggs. Add cream cheese and mix well. Divide evenly between two 9 x 13-inch baking dishes that have been prepared with nonstick cooking spray. Bake for 10–15 minutes or until eggs have completely set. Remove from dishes onto wire racks.

In a large nonstick frying pan over medium-high heat, melt butter. Add bell pepper, onion, zucchini, and mushrooms and cook until onion becomes limp. Remove from pan and set aside. Add sausage to pan and cook until lightly browned. Drain well and add bacon. Toss to mix.

In small bowl, combine cheeses. Place the first egg layer in a 9 x 13-inch baking dish that has been prepared with nonstick cooking spray. Evenly layer half of each mixture; sausage, vegetable, and cheese. Place the second egg layer in the dish and repeat with remaining mixtures. Bake lasagna in center of oven for 10–15 minutes or until cheese has melted and begins to brown. Makes 6–8 servings.

# MEXI-CALI CASSEROLE

| | |
|---:|:---|
| 1 can (15 ounces) | **black beans,** rinsed |
| 1 can (12 ounces) | **diced green chiles** |
| 1 can (6 ounces) | **sliced black olives,** drained |
| 1 | **red bell pepper,** diced |
| 4 | **scallions,** sliced |
| ½ pound | **sausage,** cooked and drained |
| 20 | **baby spinach leaves,** stemmed and chopped |
| 14 | **eggs** |
| ¾ cup | **milk** |
| | **salt and pepper,** to taste |
| 2 cups | **grated Mexican blend cheese** |
| | **salsa** |

Preheat oven to 350 degrees.

In a large bowl, combine beans, chiles, olives, bell pepper, scallions, and sausage. Pour into a 9 x 13-inch glass baking dish that has been prepared with nonstick cooking spray and spread evenly. Layer spinach leaves on sausage mixture.

In another bowl, beat eggs and milk. Add salt, pepper, and cheese; mix well and pour over spinach. Bake in center of oven until puffed, golden, and knife inserted near center comes out clean, 35–40 minutes. Serve topped with salsa. Makes 6–8 servings.

# PEEK-A-BOO EGGS

| | |
|--:|:--|
| 2 tablespoons | **butter or margarine** |
| 2 cups | **shredded hash brown potatoes** |
| | **salt and pepper,** to taste |
| 12 slices | **bacon,** cooked and crumbled |
| 12 slices | **American cheese** |
| 12 | **eggs** |
| 1 cup | **whipping cream** |

Preheat oven to 450 degrees.

In a large frying pan over medium high heat, melt butter and cook hash browns until browned and crispy, add salt and pepper. Press potatoes evenly on bottom of a 9 x 13-inch baking dish that has been prepared with nonstick cooking spray. Sprinkle with bacon and layer with cheese slices. Make a small indentation in center of cheese slices to hold eggs in place.

Crack an egg on each slice of cheese. Gently pour cream evenly over eggs. Bake until whites are completely set and yolks are as desired, 15–20 minutes. Makes 6–8 servings.

# SOUTH-OF-THE-BORDER CASSEROLE

| | |
|---:|:---|
| 12 | **eggs,** divided |
| 2¼ cups | **milk,** divided |
| 10 slices | **bacon,** cooked and crumbled |
| 3 tablespoons | **butter or margarine** |
| 3 tablespoons | **flour** |
| 1 teaspoon | **minced garlic** |
| ½ teaspoon | **chili powder,** divided |
| 1 cup | **sour cream** |
| 1½ cups | **grated Mexican blend cheese** |
| 1 cup | **salsa** |
| 1 package (24 ounces) | **shredded hash brown potatoes** |

Preheat oven to 375 degrees.

In a small bowl, beat 6 eggs with ¼ cup of milk, pour into a large frying pan over medium heat, and cook eggs, stirring frequently, until eggs have set. Transfer to a large bowl and add bacon. Set aside.

In a medium frying pan, melt butter over medium heat. Whisk in flour, garlic, and ¼ teaspoon chili powder. Add remaining milk and stir constantly until sauce thickens and begins to boil, 5–7 minutes. Add to eggs and bacon with sour cream, cheese, salsa, and hash browns. Mix well and pour into a 9 x 13-inch glass baking dish that has been prepared with nonstick cooking spray. Bake in center of oven until puffed and golden, 25–30 minutes.

Remove from oven, and using a spoon, scoop out 6 holes. Crack 1 egg into each hole and evenly sprinkle with remaining chili powder. Bake until whites are completely set and yolks are as desired, 10–15 minutes. Let stand for 5 minutes. Serve with additional salsa and sour cream. Makes 6 servings.

# QUICK AND EASY CASSEROLE

| | |
|---:|:---|
| ½ cup | **diced onion** |
| 2 tablespoons | **water** |
| ⅓ pound | **Canadian bacon,** diced |
| ½ cup | **grated cheddar cheese** |
| ½ cup | **grated Monterey Jack cheese** |
| 3 cups | **stuffing mix** |
| 5 | **eggs** |
| 2 cups | **milk** |
| ½ teaspoon | **dry mustard** |
| ½ teaspoon | **onion salt** |

In a small microwavable bowl, cook onion and water on high for 2 minutes. Drain and add bacon and cheeses. Toss to mix.

Layer stuffing along bottom of a 9 x 11-inch baking dish that has been prepared with nonstick cooking spray. Top with cheese mixture.

In a medium bowl, beat eggs, milk, mustard, and onion salt and pour over cheese mixture. Cover and refrigerate for several hours or overnight.

Preheat oven to 350 degrees.

Remove from refrigerator; uncover and let stand while oven heats. Bake in center of oven until puffed, golden, and knife inserted near center comes out clean, 45–50 minutes. Makes 6–8 servings.

# SAUSAGE BAKE

| | |
|---:|:---|
| 1 pound | **sausage** |
| 1 | **small onion,** diced |
| 16 slices | **white bread,** cubed and divided |
| 4 cups | **grated cheddar cheese** |
| 6 | **eggs** |
| 2 cups | **milk** |
| | **salt and pepper,** to taste |

In a large frying pan, cook sausage with onion until it begins to brown. Drain and set aside.

Place half of the bread cubes in bottom of a 9 x 13-inch glass baking dish that has been prepared with nonstick cooking spray. Evenly layer half the sausage and half the cheese over bread. Top with remaining bread and sausage.

In a medium bowl, beat eggs, milk, salt, and pepper. Pour over bread. Spread remaining cheese on top. Cover and refrigerate overnight.

Preheat oven to 350 degrees.

Remove from refrigerator; uncover and let stand while oven heats. Bake in center of oven until puffed, golden, and knife inserted near center comes out clean, 40–50 minutes. Let it set 5–10 minutes before serving. Makes 6–8 servings.

# FAMILY FAVORITES

# MUFFIN PANCAKES

| | |
|---:|:---|
| 1/4 teaspoon | **salt** |
| 1 cup | **flour** |
| 4 | **eggs** |
| 1 cup | **milk** |
| 1 teaspoon | **vanilla** |
| 6 teaspoons | **butter or margarine,** divided |

Preheat oven to 425 degrees.

Mix salt, flour, eggs, milk, and vanilla in blender on medium speed until well blended. Prepare a 12-cup muffin pan with nonstick cooking spray. Melt 1/2 teaspoon butter in each cup.

Pour mixture, evenly divided, into muffin cups. Bake for 15 minutes or until golden and puffy. Serve immediately with honey or syrup. Makes 12 pancakes.

# CINNAMON BREAD CUSTARD

| | |
|---:|:---|
| 8 slices | **cinnamon-raisin bread,** cut into cubes |
| 1/2 cup | **butter or margarine,** melted |
| 4 | **eggs** |
| 2 | **egg yolks** |
| 3/4 cup | **sugar** |
| 3 cups | **milk** |
| 1 cup | **whipping cream** |
| 1 tablespoon | **vanilla** |
| 1 cup | **hot water** |
| | **powdered sugar** |

In a large bowl, combine bread cubes and butter. Toss lightly to coat. Lightly prepare a 9 x 13-inch baking dish with nonstick cooking spray. Evenly distribute bread in dish.

In a large bowl, beat eggs and egg yolks. Whisk in sugar, milk, cream, and vanilla. Pour over bread cubes. Chill 2 hours or up to overnight.

Preheat oven to 350 degrees.

Place baking dish on a large baking sheet with sides. Pour the hot water onto the baking sheet. Bake 45 minutes until top is lightly browned. Cool slightly, cut into 6 squares, and top with powdered sugar. Makes 8 servings.

# SCOTCH EGGS

| | |
|---:|:---|
| 1 pound | **pork sausage** |
| 1 tablespoon | **chopped fresh parsley** |
| 1 tablespoon | **grated onion** |
| 1/4 teaspoon | **ground cinnamon** |
| 1/8 teaspoon | **ground nutmeg** |
| 4 | **hard-boiled eggs,** shelled |
| 1/2 cup | **fine dry breadcrumbs** |

Preheat oven to 350 degrees.

Combine sausage, parsley, onion, cinnamon, and nutmeg; mix well. Divide sausage mixture into 4 portions; shape into patties.

Place one egg on top of each patty, shaping the sausage mixture around egg until completely covered. Roll each sausage-covered egg in breadcrumbs. Bake for 15–20 minutes until golden brown. Makes 4 servings.

# BROCCOLI-QUICHE STUFFED PEPPERS

| | |
|---:|:---|
| 4 | **medium bell peppers,** any color |
| 1 cup | **frozen broccoli florets,** thawed and divided |
| 4 | **eggs** |
| ½ cup | **milk** |
| ½ teaspoon | **garlic powder** |
| ¼ teaspoon | **dried Italian seasoning** |

Preheat oven to 325 degrees.

Cut about ½ inch off tops of peppers; remove seeds. Place peppers upright in custard cups; place cups in baking pan.

Spoon ¼ cup broccoli into each pepper. Beat eggs, milk, garlic powder, and Italian seasoning in medium bowl until blended. Pour evenly over broccoli.

Bake in center of oven until knife inserted near center comes out clean, 60–70 minutes. Let stand 5 minutes. Makes 4 servings.

# MINI BREAKFAST PIZZAS

| | |
|---:|:---|
| 4 | **eggs,** beaten |
| ⅓ cup | **pizza sauce** |
| 2 | **English muffins,** split and toasted |
| ½ cup | **grated Italian cheese blend** |
| | **dried oregano** |

Preheat oven to 450 degrees.

Prepare a large frying pan with nonstick cooking spray; heat over medium heat until hot. Pour in eggs. As eggs begin to set, gently pull the eggs across the pan with an inverted turner, forming large soft curds. Continue cooking—pulling, lifting and folding eggs—until thickened and no visible liquid egg remains. Do not stir constantly. Remove from heat.

Spread pizza sauce evenly on muffin halves; place on baking sheet. Top with eggs and cheese, dividing evenly. Bake until cheese is melted, about 5 minutes. Sprinkle with oregano. Makes 4 servings.

# EGG AND HAM BOBOLI WITH CRANBERRY SALSA

| | |
|---:|:---|
| 1 (12-inch) | **Boboli Italian bread shell** |
| 12 | **eggs,** beaten |
| 2 cups | **diced cooked ham** |
| 1 cup | **fresh or frozen cranberries,** thawed |
| 1 | **yellow bell pepper,** chopped |
| 1/2 to 1 | **jalapeno pepper,** seeds and veins removed |
| 1/2 teaspoon | **cinnamon** |
| 1/2 | **medium red onion,** peeled and roughly chopped |
| 1/2 teaspoon | **ground cumin** |
| 1/2 teaspoon | **dried oregano** |
| 1 can (6 ounces) | **frozen orange juice concentrate,** thawed |

Preheat oven to 450 degrees. Bake bread shell for 8–10 minutes.

Prepare a large frying pan with nonstick cooking spray; heat over medium heat until hot. Pour in eggs. As eggs begin to set, gently pull the eggs across the pan with an inverted turner, forming large soft curds. Continue cooking—pulling, lifting and folding eggs—until thickened and no visible liquid egg remains. Do not stir constantly. Add ham to eggs and mix together. Leave in pan on low heat until ready to place on bread shell.

Place remaining ingredients in blender or food processor fitted with metal blade; process until ingredients are coarsely chopped. Spread salsa over bread shell. Top with egg mixture. Cut into slices and serve immediately. Makes 6 servings.

# ZUCCHINI FRITTERS

| | |
|---:|:---|
| 1 | **large zucchini,** diced |
| 8 | **green onions,** thinly sliced |
| 1 tablespoon | **olive oil** |
| 1 cup | **crumbled feta cheese** |
| 1 teaspoon | **finely chopped fresh dill** |
| ½ teaspoon | **finely chopped fresh mint** |
| ½ teaspoon | **grated lemon peel** |
| | **pepper,** to taste |
| 4 | **eggs,** separated |
| ¼ cup | **flour** |
| pinch | **salt** |
| | **vegetable oil for frying** |

Saute zucchini and onions in oil until they begin to brown. Place in bowl and stir in feta, herbs, lemon peel, and pepper. Add egg yolks and flour to zucchini mixture and stir until just blended.

In a separate bowl, beat egg whites with salt until stiff peaks form and then gently fold into zucchini mixture. Drop ¼ cup of mixture into hot frying pan with a thick layer of oil. Fritters are done when the outside is brown and the inside is moist. Makes 12–14 fritters.

# BREAKFAST ROLLS

| | |
|---:|:---|
| ½ pound | **ground sausage** |
| 6 | **eggs** |
| 6 ounces | **light cream cheese,** softened |
| 1 packet | **ranch dressing mix** |
| 1 teaspoon | **minced garlic** |
| 1½ cups | **grated cheddar cheese,** divided |
| 4 tablespoons | **milk** |
| 2 cans (13.8 ounces each) | **refrigerated pizza crusts** |

Preheat oven to 425 degrees. Brown the sausage in a large frying pan.

In a medium bowl, beat eggs and cook in a medium frying pan, stirring and scraping sides regularly, until eggs have set. In a medium bowl, mix the cream cheese, ranch, garlic, 1 cup cheese, and milk.

Spread out the pizza crusts and evenly spread the cream cheese mixture on each crust. Then sprinkle the egg and sausage evenly over the cream cheese. Roll each pizza crust along the long side into a log. Slice into ½-inch slices. Place on baking sheet and bake for 15 minutes or until golden brown.

Sprinkle the remaining ½ cup cheese evenly over each roll and return to the oven to melt, 1–2 minutes. Makes 6–8 servings.

# TASTY PARMESAN TIDBITS

| | |
|---:|:---|
| ¾ cup | **finely chopped onion** |
| 2 tablespoons | **butter or margarine** |
| 6 | **eggs** |
| 2 packages (10 ounces each) | **frozen chopped spinach,** cooked and drained |
| 1 package (6 ounces) | **herb-seasoned stuffing mix** |
| 1½ cups | **grated Parmesan cheese,** divided |

Preheat oven to 350 degrees.

In a medium frying pan, saute onion in butter until tender. In large bowl, beat eggs. Stir in onion, spinach, stuffing mix, and ½ cup cheese. Form into 1-inch balls. Roll in remaining cheese.

Bake on a baking sheet that has been prepared with nonstick cooking spray until golden brown, about 25 minutes. Makes 6–10 servings.

# EGG LOAF

| | |
|---:|:---|
| 1 package | **dry yeast** |
| 1 cup | **warm water** |
| 12 | **eggs** |
| 16 ounces | **cottage cheese,** drained |
| 2 bunches | **green onion,** sliced |
| ½ pound | **bacon,** cooked and crumbled |
| ½ pound | **diced ham** |
| 2½ cups | **flour** |
| 2 teaspoons | **salt** |
| 2 cups | **grated cheddar cheese** |

Preheat oven to 400 degrees. Dissolve yeast in warm water.

In a large bowl, beat eggs. Add yeast and mix well. Add cottage cheese, onion, bacon, ham, flour, salt, and cheddar cheese. Mix thoroughly.

Prepare two loaf pans with nonstick cooking spray and fill ¾ full. Bake for 15 minutes and then lower oven to 350 degrees for another 45 minutes or until a knife inserted in center comes out clean. Allow to set for 5 minutes before serving. Makes 10–12 servings.

# CRAB AND ASPARAGUS EGG BRAID WITH CURRY SAUCE

| | |
|---:|:---|
| 4 tablespoons | **butter or margarine,** divided |
| 2 tablespoons | **flour** |
| 1 teaspoon | **curry powder** |
| 1/2 teaspoon | **salt** |
| 1 cup | **milk** |
| 1/4 teaspoon | **hot pepper sauce** |
| 1 cup | **grated Swiss cheese,** divided |
| 1 sheet | **frozen puff pastry,** thawed |
| 8 | **cooked asparagus spears** |
| 8 | **eggs,** beaten |
| 4 ounces | **flaked crab meat** |
| 1 | **egg beaten with 1 tablespoon water** |

Preheat oven to 375 degrees. In a small saucepan, melt 2 tablespoons butter. Stir in flour, curry powder, and salt. Add milk and hot pepper sauce. Cook, stirring over medium heat until smooth and thickened. Add half the cheese. Remove from heat and set aside. Lightly prepare a baking sheet with nonstick cooking spray. Place the puff pastry on the pan and roll to a 10 x 15-inch rectangle. Place the asparagus down center of the pastry.

In a large frying pan melt the remaining butter. Add eggs and cook, gently stirring over medium heat until they just start to set. Add 1/2 cup curry sauce and remaining cheese. Cook until thickened. Gently fold in the crab meat. Place the crab mixture over the asparagus in the center of the pastry. Make cuts 2 inches long and 1 inch apart along both long edges of the pastry. Fold the strips over the filling, overlapping strips as you go to form a braid. Brush the top with the egg wash. Bake for 13–15 minutes or until pastry is golden brown. Cut slices and serve with reserved curry sauce. Makes 6–8 servings.

# FRENCH BREAD CUSTARD

| | |
|---:|:---|
| 1 loaf | **French bread** |
| 1/2 cup | **unsalted butter or margarine,** melted |
| 4 | **whole eggs** |
| 2 | **egg yolks** |
| 1/2 cup | **sugar** |
| 1/4 teaspoon | **nutmeg** |
| 1 teaspoon | **vanilla** |
| 3 cups | **milk** |
| 1 cup | **whipping cream** |
| | **hot water** |
| | **powdered sugar** |
| | **fresh fruit** |
| | **maple syrup** |

Remove crust from the French bread and cut into 1 1/2-inch slices. Brush both sides of the bread with butter. Arrange the bread in a 9 x 13-inch baking dish.

Beat the eggs and yolks together; add sugar and nutmeg, whisking well to combine. Add vanilla, milk, and cream. Whisk well. Pour the custard over the bread. Refrigerate overnight.

Preheat oven to 350 degrees.

Place the custard dish into a larger baking dish. Pour hot water into the larger dish until half-way up the sides. Bake for 45 minutes or until lightly browned and puffy. Dust with powdered sugar, garnish with fresh fruit, and serve with maple syrup. Makes 8 servings.

# DESSERTS

# HOT CHOCOLATE SOUFFLE

| | |
|---:|:---|
| 1/2 cup | **sugar,** divided |
| 1/3 cup | **unsweetened cocoa powder** |
| 1/4 cup | **flour** |
| 1/8 teaspoon | **salt** |
| 1 cup | **milk** |
| 1/2 teaspoon | **vanilla** |
| 4 | **eggs,** room temperature and separated |
| 1/2 teaspoon | **cream of tartar** |

Preheat oven to 350 degrees.

Mix 1/4 cup sugar, cocoa powder, flour, and salt in medium saucepan; gradually whisk in milk until smooth. Cook over medium heat, stirring constantly, until mixture thickens and boils. Stir in vanilla. Remove from heat.

Beat egg whites and cream of tartar in mixer bowl with whisk attachment on high speed until foamy. Beating constantly, add remaining sugar, 2 tablespoons at a time, beating after each addition until sugar is dissolved.* Continue beating until whites are glossy and stand in soft peaks.

Stir egg yolks into cocoa mixture until blended. Gently but thoroughly fold yolk mixture into whites until no streaks of white remain. Carefully pour into an ungreased 2-quart souffle dish.

Bake until souffle is puffy, delicately browned, and shakes slightly when oven rack is moved gently back and forth, 30–40 minutes. Serve immediately. Makes 6 servings.

*Rub a bit of mixture between thumb and forefinger; it should feel completely smooth.

# CLASSIC FLAN

| | |
|---:|:---|
| ½ cup | **sugar** |
| 1 can (14 ounces) | **sweetened condensed milk** |
| 1 can (12 ounces) | **evaporated milk** |
| 6 | **eggs** |
| ½ teaspoon | **vanilla** |
| | **hot water** |

Preheat oven to 350 degrees.

Place sugar in small heavy saucepan. Heat over medium heat, watching carefully, until sugar is melted and turns deep golden brown. Immediately remove from heat and pour into a 9-inch flan dish or pie plate. Holding dish with potholders, quickly tilt dish to coat bottom completely and evenly. Syrup will harden quickly.

Combine milks in medium saucepan; heat until very hot. Milk should be steaming but not bubbling. Meanwhile beat eggs and vanilla in medium bowl until blended but not foamy; slowly stir in hot milk.

Place flan dish in baking pan large enough to hold dish without touching sides of pan. Pour egg mixture into flan dish.

Place pan on rack in center oven; pour very hot water into baking pan to within ½ inch of top of flan dish. Bake until knife inserted near center comes out clean, 35–40 minutes. Remove dish from water at once; cool on wire rack. Makes 6–8 servings.

# BANANAS FOSTER CHEESE PIE

| | |
|---:|:---|
| 2 tablespoons | **butter or margarine** |
| 2½ cups | **sliced bananas** |
| 1¼ cups | **sugar,** divided |
| 3 tablespoons | **fresh lemon juice,** divided |
| 1 teaspoon | **pumpkin pie spice** |
| 1 (9-inch) | **graham cracker piecrust** |
| 2 packages (8 ounces each) | **cream cheese,** softened |
| 6 | **eggs,** room temperature |
| 1½ teaspoons | **vanilla** |
| ⅓ cup | **flour** |

Preheat oven to 350 degrees.

Heat butter in large frying pan over medium heat. Add bananas; cook, stirring gently, until soft, about 2 minutes. Do not mash. Add ¼ cup sugar, 1½ tablespoons lemon juice, and pie spice. Cook, stirring gently, until mixture thickens, about 1 minute. Spread evenly in bottom of piecrust.

Combine cream cheese, eggs, remaining sugar, remaining lemon juice, and vanilla in mixer bowl. Beat on high speed until well blended. Reduce speed to low. Beat in flour just until blended and no streaks of flour remain. Pour over banana mixture.

Carefully place pie on rack in center of oven. Bake until knife inserted midway between center and edge of pie comes out clean, 40–45 minutes. Cool completely on wire rack. Refrigerate, loosely covered, until firm, several hours or overnight. Makes 8 servings.

# CREAM PUFF DESSERT

| | |
|---:|:---|
| ½ cup | **butter or margarine** |
| 1 cup | **water** |
| 1 cup | **flour** |
| 4 | **eggs** |
| 1 package (6 ounces) | **instant vanilla pudding** |
| 3 cups | **milk** |
| 1 package (8 ounces) | **cream cheese,** softened |
| 2 cups | **frozen whipped topping,** thawed |
| | **chocolate syrup,** to taste |

Preheat oven to 400 degrees.

Bring butter and water to a boil. Blend in flour, beating it into a ball. Add eggs one at a time and beat well. Spread mixture into a 9 x 13-inch glass baking dish that has been prepared with nonstick cooking spray and bake for 40 minutes. Cool crust.

Mix pudding, milk, and cream cheese together. Spread over cooled crust. Top with whipped topping. Drizzle chocolate syrup over the top. Keep refrigerated. Makes 8–12 servings.

# BAKED CUSTARD

|            |                    |
|-----------:|--------------------|
| 4          | **eggs**           |
| ½ cup      | **sugar**          |
| 1 teaspoon | **vanilla**        |
| ¼ teaspoon | **salt**           |
| 2½ cups    | **milk,** scalded  |
| ¼ teaspoon | **cinnamon**       |

Preheat oven to 350 degrees.

Beat together eggs, sugar, vanilla, and salt. Stir in milk. Pour into a 2-quart baking dish that has been prepared with nonstick cooking spray. Sprinkle with cinnamon. Place in the oven for 35–40 minutes. When done, the custard should be firm, but gel-like. Makes 6–8 servings.

# FROZEN VANILLA CUSTARD ICE CREAM

| | |
|---:|:---|
| 6 | **eggs** |
| 3/4 cup | **sugar** |
| 2 tablespoons | **honey** |
| 1/4 teaspoon | **salt** |
| 2 cups | **milk** |
| 2 cups | **whipping cream** |
| 1 tablespoon | **vanilla** |
| | **crushed ice** |
| | **rock salt** |

Beat eggs, sugar, honey, and salt in medium heavy saucepan until blended; stir in milk. Cook over low heat, stirring constantly, until mixture is just thick enough to coat a metal spoon with a thin film and temperature reaches 160 degrees,* about 15 minutes. Do not allow to boil. Remove from heat immediately. Cool quickly—set pan in larger pan of ice water; stir occasionally and gently for a few minutes to hasten cooling. Press piece of plastic wrap onto surface of custard. Refrigerate until thoroughly chilled, at least 1 hour.

Pour chilled custard, whipping cream, and vanilla into 1-gallon ice cream freezer can. Freeze according to manufacturer's directions, using 6 parts crushed ice to 1 part rock salt. Transfer to freezer containers, allowing head space for expansion; freeze until firm. Makes 1 1/2–2 quarts.

*Use a candy thermometer.

# EGGNOG BREAD PUDDING

| | |
|---:|:---|
| ¾ pound | **loaf white bread** |
| 1 cup | **semisweet chocolate chips** |
| 2 cups | **eggnog** |
| 1 cup | **half-and-half** |
| ⅓ cup | **sugar** |
| 6 | **eggs** |
| 3 tablespoons | **butter or margarine,** cut into small pieces |
| | **hot water** |
| | **powdered sugar,** to taste |

Heat oven to 325 degrees. Prepare a 9 x 13-inch baking dish with nonstick cooking spray. Cut bread into 1-inch cubes and coarsely chop chocolate chips.

In baking dish, toss bread and chocolate. In large bowl, whisk eggnog, half-and-half, sugar, and eggs until well mixed. Pour eggnog mixture over bread and chocolate; dot with butter. Set baking dish in large roasting pan; place on middle oven rack. Fill roasting pan with hot water to come halfway up side of baking dish. Bake bread pudding 1 hour or until knife inserted in center comes out clean. Sprinkle with powdered sugar. Serve pudding warm. Makes 8–12 servings.

# RASPBERRY-DARK CHOCOLATE BRULEE

| | |
|---:|:---|
| 1 ½ cups | **whipping cream** |
| 1 cup | **semisweet chocolate chips** |
| 1 cup | **dark chocolate chips** |
| 2 | **eggs** |
| 2 tablespoons | **brown sugar** |
| 1 tablespoon | **raspberry extract** |
| 1 teaspoon | **vanilla** |
| | **pinch of salt** |
| 6 teaspoons | **sugar** |

In a saucepan, heat cream until it almost begins to boil. Remove from heat.

In a blender, mix remaining ingredients except for sugar, about 30 seconds. With the blender running on low, slowly pour in hot cream and blend for 1 minute. Pour mixture into 6 personal-size serving dishes. Refrigerate until set, approximately 30 minutes. Sprinkle the top of each dish with about 1 teaspoon sugar and brulee top with torch. Makes 6 servings.

# VANILLA CREMEUX

| | |
|---:|:---|
| 1 cup | **sugar** |
| 8 | **egg yolks** |
| | **pinch of salt** |
| 2 cups | **whipping cream** |
| 1 tablespoon | **vanilla** |
| 1½ tablespoons | **gelatin** |
| 4 teaspoons | **water** |

In a large bowl, mix sugar, eggs, and salt. Set aside. In a saucepan, bring cream and vanilla almost to a boil. Slowly add to the egg mixture and blend. Return to pan and cook, stirring constantly, until it reaches 176 degrees.* Remove from heat.

In a small bowl, mix gelatin and water and let sit for 5 minutes and then melt in a microwave for 15 seconds. Add gelatin to egg mixture and stir. Pour through a strainer to remove any small particles. Pour into 6 ramekins and freeze. Thaw before serving. Makes 6 servings.

*Use a candy thermometer.

# CUSTARD CUP SUNDAES

| | |
|---:|:---|
| 1 box (3.9 ounces) | **instant pudding,** any flavor, sugar free works well |
| 6 teaspoons | **butter,** divided |
| 4 | **eggs** |
| 1 cup | **milk** |
| 6 tablespoons | **flour** |
| 1/2 teaspoon | **vanilla** |
| 1 small container (8 ounces) | **frozen whipped topping,** thawed |
| 6 | **maraschino cherries** |
| 1 | **banana,** sliced |

Preheat oven to 450 degrees. Prepare the pudding according to directions and chill.

Place 1 teaspoon of the butter in each of 6 ramekins. Place into oven and melt butter. Tilt ramekins so butter is completely covering cup bottoms and sides. Set aside.

Beat together eggs, milk, flour, and vanilla. Pour about 1/3 cup batter into each hot ramekin, making a small indentation in the center. Bake for 8 minutes. Reduce oven to 375 degrees and bake another 8 minutes. Take ramekins out of oven and let cool for 5 minutes.

Fill ramekins with pudding. Top with whipped topping and garnish with cherries and sliced bananas. Makes 6 servings.

# NOTES

## METRIC CONVERSION CHART

| Volume Measurements | | Weight Measurements | | Temperature Conversion | |
| --- | --- | --- | --- | --- | --- |
| U.S. | Metric | U.S. | Metric | Fahrenheit | Celsius |
| 1 teaspoon | 5 ml | ½ ounce | 15 g | 250 | 120 |
| 1 tablespoon | 15 ml | 1 ounce | 30 g | 300 | 150 |
| ¼ cup | 60 ml | 3 ounces | 90 g | 325 | 160 |
| ⅓ cup | 75 ml | 4 ounces | 115 g | 350 | 180 |
| ½ cup | 125 ml | 8 ounces | 225 g | 375 | 190 |
| ⅔ cup | 150 ml | 12 ounces | 350 g | 400 | 200 |
| ¾ cup | 175 ml | 1 pound | 450 g | 425 | 220 |
| 1 cup | 250 ml | 2¼ pounds | 1 kg | 450 | 230 |

 Check out these "101" favorites
for more tasty recipes:

| | |
|---|---|
| **Cake Mix** | **More Slow Cooker** |
| **More Cake Mix** | **BBQ** |
| **Chocolate** | **Casserole** |
| **Gelatin** | **Dutch Oven** |
| **Yogurt** | **Blender** |
| **Pudding** | **Toaster Oven** |
| **Mac & Cheese** | **Chicken** |
| **Ramen Noodles** | **Rotisserie Chicken** |
| **Salad** | **Ground Beef** |
| **Zucchini** | **Meatballs** |
| **Tofu** | **Grits** |
| **Tortilla** | **Potato** |
| **Canned Biscuits** | **Cheese** |
| **Canned Soup** | **More Ramen** |
| **Slow Cooker** | |

Each 128 pages, $9.99

Available at bookstores or directly
from GIBBS SMITH
1.800.835.4993
www.gibbs-smith.com

# ABOUT THE AUTHOR

Toni Patrick is the culinary creative behind *101 Things to Do with Ramen Noodles, 101 Things to Do with Mac and Cheese, 101 Things to Do with Canned Biscuits, 101 Things to Do with a Blender,* and *101 More Things to Do with Ramen Noodles.* She has been featured on the Food Network. She lives in Walden, Colorado, with her daughter, Robbi.